THE WAR OF 1812

BY PETER I. BOSCO

THE MILLBROOK
PRESS

BROOKFIELD,
CONNECTICUT

Maps by Frank Senyk

Photographs and illustrations courtesy of the National Archives:
pp. 11, 25, 27; North Wind Picture Archives: pp. 18, 115; Culver
Pictures: pp. 19, 50, 52, 58; Anne S. K. Brown Military Collection,
Brown University Library: p. 28; Bettmann Archive: pp. 30, 45, 101,
112; U.S. Naval Academy Museum: pp. 34, 35, 66, 73, 85; Independence National Historical Park Collection: p. 46; National Archives of
Canada: pp. 61, 82; Massachusetts Historical Society: p. 69; Indiana
Historical Society (Negative No. C199): p. 83; Library of Congress:
pp. 87, 89, 94; The Peale Museum, Baltimore City Life Museums:
p. 96; National Museum of American Art, Washington, D.C./
Art Resource, NY: p. 111.

Cataloging-in-Publication Data
Bosco, Peter I.
The War of 1812 / by Peter I. Bosco.
p. cm.—
Bibliography p.
Summary: Describes causes of the war and tells of various events
and battles.
ISBN 1-56294-004-X
1. United States—History—1812–1815, War of 1812. 2. Naval
battles. 3. Sea Power. 4. Privateering. I. Title.
973.5 1991

CONTENTS

As a young boy, I spent hours playing Broadsides, *Milton Bradley's long out-of-print War of 1812 board game, with my best friend William Rachunas. That was my first exposure to this wonderful but often neglected period of American history.*

I dedicate this book to Bill.

CHAPTER 1

CLASH AT SEA

"Sail ho!" yelled the lookout from the crow's nest of the British frigate *Macedonian.*

"Can you make her out?" replied an officer from the deck below.

"Looks like a frigate, sir," the lookout yelled down, "off the port bow."

In the era of wooden ships, a frigate was a three-masted warship armed with between 30 and 50 guns. Only two years old, the 38-gun *Macedonian* herself was a fine and modern frigate, one of the best in the Royal Navy. She had been cruising in the Atlantic, some six hundred miles west of the Canary Islands, when the mysterious frigate appeared.

"There's an unidentified vessel bearing to port," barked the officer on deck to the sailor next to him. "Inform the captain." Below deck the ship's commander, Captain John S. Carden, was studying nautical maps.

"Begging the Captain's pardon, sir," said the English seaman as he saluted, "an unknown ship is approaching us." Captain Carden leaned forward in his seat.

"Is she American?" he asked, in a wishful tone of voice. For the year was 1812. America had just gone to war with the British Empire. The captains of Britain's venerable warships were eager to pummel the tiny American Navy. Each skipper wanted to capture an American ship to sail back to England as his "prize," a trophy of war.

"Don't know, Captain," replied the seaman. "She's showin' no colors." Captain Carden sprang from his chair. He grabbed his telescope and ran to the main (top) deck. He extended the cylindrical spyglass and took a hard look at the approaching vessel. The ship's flag had not yet been raised, but Captain Carden smiled.

"She's a Yankee frigate," he said to a lieutenant standing next to him. "Give the order to clear the decks for action."

Captain Carden was familiar with every frigate the Americans had. (There were only seven of them.) Although three of them mounted more guns than the 38-gun *Macedonian,* he confidently believed that his ship could lick any ship in the U.S. Navy.

"Battle stations," cried the lieutenant. Sailors scurried about to the blast of bugles and the beat of drums as the *Macedonian* prepared for action. Tubs of water were laid out in case the ship caught fire. Sand was strewn on the decks so that they would not become slippery with blood. The ship's carpenters laid out wooden plugs of various sizes that could be used to seal off cannonball holes in the hull.

Naval soldiers, called marines, assembled on the main deck where they were issued pistols, cutlasses, and pikes. A lieutenant of the Royal Marines gave them instructions on boarding tactics. Marine sharpshooters climbed to the tops of masts, from where they could pick off seamen on the enemy's deck when the ships closed in.

Most important, the gunners had to get ready. Like all frigates, the *Macedonian*'s main battery was just below the main deck. The walls of the gun deck were lined with hatches called gun ports, through which the cannons fired. (In those days a ship had to face sideways to shoot most of its guns.)

The *Macedonian*'s gun ports swung open. From her belly sprang the menacing snouts of her slender cannons. Each weighed more than a ton and had a crew of eight tough, well-muscled men. Past the muzzles of their cannons the British gunners saw the ship whose identity was still unknown to them.

"Think she's American?" asked a gunner.

"We'll know once she's in range," replied another. "And if she is, we'll blow her out of the water!"

Not all of the sailors on board the *Macedonian* were as enthusiastic. Some of the crewmen were Americans. They had been forcibly "impressed" by Captain Carden to serve aboard his ship as virtual slaves. Only by the impressment of American sailors could Britain's naval captains keep their ships fully crewed. American outrage over this despicable but all too common practice by the British was one of the main reasons the two countries were at war.

When the American frigate came within a mile, it at last raised the Stars and Stripes. Now the *Macedonian*'s whole crew knew that they were about to face their first battle against an American warship. A minute later, a group of impressed American sailors approached Captain Carden.

"Begging your pardon, sir," one American seaman said respectfully, "we can't fight against our own people." The stone-hearted skipper gave them a cold stare.

"Get to your battle stations, every one of you," shouted Captain Carden, "or I'll have you shot." He turned and ordered an officer to go below deck and shoot any man who tried to desert his duty.

As the two ships neared each other, an eerie silence fell over the gun deck of the *Macedonian*. The gunners peered through their gun ports waiting for the order to shoot. Suddenly, orange flame and gray smoke spewed from the gun ports of the American frigate as it fired the first broadside.

"Fire!" bellowed a British gunnery officer. The *Macedonian* thundered and shook as it unleashed a return broadside. The big guns lurched backward in recoil until they were stopped by the breach ropes, which were cables anchored to the ship's hull. While they reloaded their cannons, the gunners heard the rumble of another broadside from the American ship. They heard the sound of breaking timbers above—but the gun deck had not been hit.

"Fire!" bellowed the gunnery officer. The breach ropes made a sound like a whip as they caught the violent recoil of the guns. The gunners again reloaded, then laboriously maneuvered their cannons back into firing position.

"Fire!" bellowed the gunnery officer. By now the gun deck had become hazy with smoke. The sulfurous odor of burned gunpowder made the gunners' noses wrinkle and their eyes water while they reloaded once again.

"Fire!" bellowed the gunnery officer.

The ships had come within a thousand yards of each other. Captain Carden now knew that the ship with which the *Macedonian* was furiously exchanging broadsides was the 44-gun *United States,* commanded by Captain Stephen Decatur. The two ships had met once, in Norfolk, Virginia, before the war. While in port there, Captain Carden met with Captain Decatur. The two captains joked about the possibility of war. Each insisted to the other that his ship would emerge the victor if they ever met in battle.

It was still too early to tell who would come out on top, but Captain Carden was getting worried. The *Macedonian*'s masts and sails were taking a beating. He was amazed by the speed and accuracy of the American gunners. (Unlike the Royal Navy, the U.S. Navy had made gun drills, target practice, and precision artillery tactics top priorities.)

As the battle raged on, Captain Carden belatedly realized that his best chance was to bring the *Macedonian* close enough to use its carronades. These were stubby, wide-mouth guns that fired massive thirty-six-pound cannonballs. The four-foot-long iron monsters were the ship's battering rams, but they were only effective at ranges under 150 yards or so.

The British skipper ordered the helmsman to close on the American frigate, now about three hundred yards away.

The United States *(right) defeating the* Macedonian.

The ship's ability to maneuver, however, was hampered by the extensive damage the American ship had dealt to the *Macedonian*'s rigging. The highly trained American gunners had shot off the ship's mizzen gaff, jib boom, two top yards, half the bowsprit, and part of the spanker.

Unable to get his ship any closer, Captain Carden knew that the battle had turned against him. Yet to the men below deck, things did not seem that bad. The gun deck was undamaged for the most part. The gunners could not see that the *Macedonian*'s rigging was fast becoming a hopeless snare of splintered masts, tangled ropes, and torn canvas.

At one point some British gunners looked out the gun ports to see the *United States* in a shroud of flame and smoke. "She's afire!" yelled one. A wild cheer broke out along the *Macedonian*'s gun deck. "The enemy's afire!" yelled another gunner. "The day is ours."

But the British had not won. The blaze aboard the *United States* was an optical illusion caused by the rapid succession of her broadsides. The crack American gunners were getting off two shots for every one British.

Aboard the *United States,* the American skipper had been instructing his gunners to shoot at the *Macedonian's* rigging. Once Captain Decatur saw that it had become a mass of wreckage, he knew it was time to start working on the enemy's hull. "Aim for the gun deck," he now ordered his gunners, "she needs a little hulling."

A minute later the men on the *Macedonian's* gun deck felt their ship shake from end to end as if Neptune himself had bashed them with a giant sledgehammer. One murderous American broadside after another slammed into the British ship.

Cannonballs crashed through the *Macedonian's* timbers. Splinters flew everywhere. The sound of breaking beams mingled with the cries of the wounded. As the surgeon's bay overflowed, gun crews were reduced to two or three men.

Then the pounding stopped. The dazed British gunners looked out, but the *United States* was nowhere in sight. They all knew what was coming.

The *United States,* which still had most of its rigging intact, had managed to swing its side in front of the *Macedonian's* bow. This deadly maneuver was called "crossing the T." From this position the *United States* could rake the length of the British ship with a concentrated broadside but would be out of reach of the *Macedonian's* side-mounted guns. Below deck the British seamen waited for the final death blow.

That broadside never came. Captain Carden knew it was all over. He ordered the colors struck. Down fluttered the battle-tattered Union Jack. The British had suffered 104 casualties in the two-hour duel. A dozen Americans were killed or wounded.

Soon, the British officers came alongside the *United States* in a rowboat. Captain Carden, a broken man, handed over his sword and scabbard. (This was the traditional gesture of defeat.) Captain Decatur reached out his hand to greet the British skipper, not as a beaten foe but as a naval captain with whom he had been friendly in Norfolk.

For the impressed American sailors aboard the *Macedonian*, the victory of the *United States* brought jubilation. It meant an end to their slavery and a return to their homes.

The *Macedonian* was now a prize of war. Although smashed, she was still seaworthy. After lashing the two ships together, American seamen and carpenters worked on the *Macedonian* for two weeks, plugging holes, patching the sails, and making other temporary repairs.

A "prize crew" was then sent over to run the British warship. At first the British sailors feared the American officers and seamen. They soon found they had nothing to fear. In fact, life under the Americans was more pleasant than it had been under their British officers. The British enlisted men also noticed that the American sailors seemed happier and more satisfied.

The British soon realized that this was because the Americans had something to fight for. The British sailors fought because they had been ordered to. If Britain had cause in this conflict, it was a mystery to them. They were told merely that the two countries were at war and never told why. They saw that the American seamen knew exactly why they fought. They were fighting for freedom of the seas.

Why was this such a sensitive issue to the Americans? How had the United States gotten into another struggle against the English less than thirty years after the Revolution that had won their independence? Were other factors involved? What could have been so important to cause America to take on Britain, the most powerful country on earth? To fully understand the answer to these questions requires a look back to what had happened to the young Republic since the end of the Revolution.

A NEW
REPUBLIC

The European countries had been amazed by the success of the American Revolution. Yet few in Europe expected the United States to survive as a nation. The demands of war had managed to temporarily unite the thirteen colonies, Europeans believed, but peace would surely bring disunity and quarreling between the states.

If Europeans believed that the Union would soon fall apart, so did many Americans. The Articles of Confederation, which loosely bound the thirteen states together, were not strong enough to keep them united in peace. Under the Articles, the central government consisted mainly of a weak Continental Congress. Each of the states practically ruled itself.

Even George Washington feared for the country's survival and blamed the different state governments for growing disorder. Many people began to think that it was just a matter of time until the cracks in the United States' brittle union caused it to break up into separate countries. A lack of economic cooperation between the states—or even a national currency—had caused a depression. Many people were out of work; meanwhile, prices were rising rapidly. The new nation was nearly bankrupt. A spirit of unrest and general lawlessness began to grow.

A serious blow to American unity came in 1786, just three years after the end of the Revolution. Daniel Shays, a former Continental Army captain who had fought at Bunker Hill, led disgruntled Massachusetts farmers in a revolt to protest the state's heavy taxes and fiscal policy. Although armed, Shays and his followers were essentially nonviolent. The nervous Massachusetts government leaders, however, used the state militia to crush what became known as Shays' Rebellion.

Massachusetts had appealed to the Continental Congress for help, but the virtually powerless Congress was unable to give any. The weakness of the Articles of Confederation was becoming more and more apparent. Even staunch advocates of states' rights began to recognize the need for a strong central government.

Not all America's troubles were domestic, either. Far away, in the Mediterranean Sea, American merchant ships were learning the price of independence.

In those days, the waters of the western Mediterranean Sea were "patrolled" by four North African Muslim states (Algiers, Tunis, Tripoli, and Morocco) situated on what was called the Barbary Coast. The pashas (rulers) of the Barbary States were in fact lords of piracy. Each had a fleet of pirate ships that scoured the sea in search of merchant ships to capture. Sometimes a captured ship would be added to the pirate fleet, but usually it could be bought back by the country that lost it. Its cargo was seldom recovered. Its unlucky crew was enslaved or imprisoned until ransom was paid.

All countries whose ships sailed those waters were required to make annual payments, called tribute, to the Barbary States. It was what today might be called a protection racket. The amount and method of payment were arranged by treaty. Even if a country had a treaty, Barbary pirates would attack that country's ships if the tribute was late or not enough, or if they were simply in the mood.

Generally, the weaker the country, the more tribute it paid, and the more its ships were attacked anyway.

Even Britain, with its powerful Navy, paid a modest tribute—it was cheaper than going to war. In addition, the British kept a squadron of warships in the Mediterranean to enforce the safe passage of their merchant vessels, even though that was supposedly guaranteed by treaty.

Before the Revolution, colonial American merchant ships were sheltered from the marauding North Africans by the broad sail of the Royal Navy. By 1785, Britain had made sure that the Barbary pashas realized that British protection no longer extended to ships from America. That year Algerine cruisers captured two American vessels.

Without the British Navy to protect them, American merchant ships soon became a favorite target of Barbary pirates. (The powerful pashas considered the United States such a despicably weak nation that they never bothered to formally declare war.) Since the Continental Congress did not have the power to tax, it had no funds to build a navy. Nor could it pay tribute. Nor could it raise the ransom for American sailors languishing in Barbary dungeons or slaving in Algerine quarries.

These reasons and others were motivation for the Constitutional Convention, which met in Philadelphia on May 25, 1787, to create a new government. From this historic gathering came the U.S. Constitution, which has remained the foundation of American government for more than two centuries.

With increased federal powers, Congress soon established tariffs (taxes on imported goods) that favored American shipping. This not only improved the U.S. economy but also generated revenue for the government. Americans began to prosper, too. Agriculture and manufacturing began to flourish. Goods and services flowed between the states in an orderly fashion. A national economy was beginning to emerge.

Again Europe was amazed. Not only had the upstart Americans survived the Revolution—now they were overcoming the greater challenge of living together peacefully. But the new nation's troubles were far from over.

FRICTION IN THE NORTH AND WEST

In the years after the Revolution, American dislike and distrust of Britain persisted. One source of friction was British rule in Canada. The boundary had supposedly been settled in 1783, but details of the agreement were vague. A more important source of dispute was the fate of the unsettled areas of the Northwest—the area that today is called the Midwest.

When the United States was founded, there were only a handful of American settlers beyond the Ohio River. This rich area, which included the present-day states of Ohio, Indiana, Illinois, Michigan, and Wisconsin, was the home of many Indian tribes. The British had agreed that the whole area would belong to the United States. They also agreed to withdraw their troops from a line of outposts along the southern rim of the Great Lakes.

The British did not pull their troops out, however. They wanted to keep control of the lucrative Indian fur trade, and some British officials hoped that continued occupation might make possible a readjustment of the boundary in their favor.

British agents also encouraged Indian tribes to resist the advance of American settlers. In the years after the Revolution, American pioneers trekked over the Appalachian Mountains into the Ohio Valley in ever-increasing numbers. (Between 1783 and 1812, the population of Kentucky rose from 12,000 to 400,000.) Despite Indian resistance, settlers pushed past the Ohio River. By 1810 the population of Ohio would reach over 230,000, and thousands of others would press on to Indiana and Illinois.

Americans resented Britain's occupation of the Northwest outposts. They also hated the British for stirring up the Indians. This kept alive the terrible memory of American pioneers who were slaughtered in Anglo-Indian raids during the War of Independence.

Events in Europe soon increased tensions between Britain and the United States. In 1792 there began a series of

Ohio Valley settlers faced a hard life in the wild.

bloody struggles called the Napoleonic Wars (after Napoleon I, emperor of the French). With only two brief rests, Britain would be at war with France for the next twenty-three years. The United States was officially neutral, but it would be drawn into conflict with both countries.

Immediately after war broke out in Europe, Britain tried to sever overseas trade between France and its colonies in the West Indies by blockading ports and intercepting ships. A way for the French to get around this blockade was to channel their trade to neutral ports in the United States. Then the goods would continue on as U.S. exports. American merchant ships, eager to get in on the lucrative West Indies trade, flocked to take the place of French vessels.

The British were not fooled for long, and British captains were ordered to seize American ships that engaged in this trade. Along with a flare-up of fighting between settlers and British-supported Indians in the Northwest, this inflamed feeling against the British. Many Americans called for war with Britain.

TROUBLE AT SEA American ships were being threatened increasingly by the Barbary pirates, too. The British encouraged Algiers, the most aggressive of the lot, to prey on Britain's commercial rivals; and the United States was now one of those rivals.

America had a long coastline, many natural ports, vast forests, and a seafaring tradition inherited from England. Because of this, shipping and shipbuilding had developed well before the Revolution. To the British, that had been fine while America was still a colony. But as the U.S. shipping industry began to boom after the Revolution, they saw a threat to their own maritime supremacy. In a way, the pirates became a useful economic weapon for Britain. A saying among London merchants went: "If there were no Algiers, it would be worth England's while to build one."[1]

New York City's busy harbor in the days of sail.

The American government found, however, that the Barbary States could be bought off. Congress decided that this was the easiest way out of a difficult situation and cheaper than building a navy. Congress also knew that Britain might feel even more threatened if the United States started building warships. It did not want to aggravate the already sensitive relations between the two nations.

So American sea captains delivered gifts and tribute to Algiers and the other states in exchange for passage of American ships in the Mediterranean Sea. Congress authorized money for this purpose as part of the national budget. Every year more was demanded. This was complicated by rivalry among the pashas over who would receive the largest tribute, and punctuated by the occasional capture of an American merchant ship.

In 1792, as tension with Britain increased over the West Indies trade, Algiers was also acting up. Congress debated whether to pay tribute or go to war. The argument for the war was pointless, however, since there was no navy with which to fight one. Instead, Congress raised $2,000 ransoms for each imprisoned American sailor and decided to negotiate another treaty of tribute with the pashas.

Despite these blackmail payments, the Algerines seized eleven American merchant ships the very next year. The American government protested, but diplomatic protests were little comfort to the owners of the hijacked ships and stolen cargo. Nor did they satisfy the families of the imprisoned sailors, who faced a life of toil in the stone quarries of Algiers with iron shackles on their feet and bread and vinegar once a day.

Confronted with bitter accusations from the public that the government was not doing its constitutional duty to "provide for the common defense," Congress finally authorized the construction of six frigates in 1794. Some Congressmen still feared that building warships might somehow get the United States into a conflict with Britain. But that year tensions between the two nations eased.

JAY'S TREATY One reason for the easing tensions was that peace came to the Northwest. Disturbed by British and Indian activity, President George Washington sent the U.S. Army into Ohio. The expedition was commanded by the Revolutionary War hero General Anthony Wayne. He had about 2,000 regulars (full-time professional Army men) and 1,000 mounted Kentucky volunteers. On August 20, 1794, they reached a patch of forest on the Maumee River (fifteen miles from present-day Toledo) where a hurricane had blown down most of the trees.

There, General Wayne and his men met a war party of some 2,000 Indians and 70 white men, mostly British. The fight that followed climaxed with a bayonnet charge personally led by General Wayne. The Indian force was routed after the Americans killed many warriors and eight chiefs. A crushing defeat for the Northwest Indians, the Battle of Fallen Timbers was followed shortly by a peace treaty.

Britain withdrew support for the Indians for the time being. Also in 1794, President Washington sent Chief Justice John Jay to London as a special envoy to settle disputes over maritime trade and Canada. The British said they would still seize American ships believed to be carrying contraband goods to France. But they signed a treaty agreeing to lift some restrictions on American trade with the West Indies. Moreover, they agreed to hand over all of the Northwest ports and outposts to the United States.

Jay's Treaty brought good relations between the two countries to a peak. Many Americans, however, attacked the treaty as a "sellout" because it didn't take a firmer stand on America's rights as a neutral country in the war with France. Yet it achieved all that a weak country could reasonably expect. Settling some matters was surely wiser than settling none at all. Above all, Jay's Treaty avoided war with Britain.

The next year (1795), a new treaty was signed with Algiers. The United States paid stiff ransoms for some 115 American sailors, agreed to higher annual tribute, and even built a 36-gun frigate as a gift to the pasha (which was used, of course, for further piracy). Altogether, this peace package cost Americans $992,462.25.

This was more than it would cost to complete the six frigates begun the year before. Yet with the new treaties with Britain and Algiers, it no longer seemed necessary to have a navy, which would be expensive to maintain, supply, and man. So Congress halted construction on the six frigates and congratulated itself on having saved money.

But while the ships sat half-built at shipyards in Philadelphia, Boston, and Norfolk, trouble was brewing with France. And the United States would find, as well, that its troubles with the Barbary pirates were just beginning.

CHAPTER 3

FREEDOM OF THE SEAS

The French were outraged by Jay's Treaty. They had been America's allies in the War of Independence, and they considered that alliance to be still in effect. Accordingly, the United States should declare war on Britain.

The United States claimed that its earlier alliance had been made with the king of France and, since he had been overthrown in 1789 and guillotined by revolutionaries, it was no longer valid. The new French Republic that replaced the monarchy had a violent, lawless, and ugly side, and the United States government was not anxious to associate America with it.

Still, the French felt that the Americans were ungrateful for all France had done for them during the War of Independence. Jay's Treaty had also come at a time when poor harvests had made France depend heavily on grain shipments from the United States, and the treaty made no exception for foodstuffs. In retaliation, France gave its sea captains the authority, in 1797, to seize any American merchant ship carrying food or any other goods to England.

Congress now approved long-overdue funding for the six half-completed frigates and for the purchase or construction of more ships. Over the next year, while the United States was assembling a fleet of fighting ships as fast as it could, some three hundred American merchant vessels were seized by the French. The American crews were often left to fend for themselves on the closest beach while their ship was auctioned off at the nearest French port. The American skippers protested to their captors, but they knew their argument was useless because America had no navy to give point to it.

It didn't matter to the captors that their country was not at war with the United States. Why should their government bother to declare war on a nation of backwoods farmers too weak to protect their oceangoing vessels? It was a primal law that the strong take what they will, and the weak suffer what they must.

President John Adams made a final attempt to reason with France. He sent a commission to Paris to discuss a just and peaceful settlement. The French officials, identified only as Monsieurs X, Y, and Z, would not open negotiations until they received a bribe of $250,000. The insulted American commissioners refused and sailed back to Washington.

The news of the "XYZ Affair" outraged the American public. The popular slogan became "Millions for defense, but not one cent for tribute."[2] On April 30, 1798, Congress created the United States Navy and Marine Corps.

President Adams declared a policy of "armed neutrality" and authorized the Navy to capture French warships wherever found. In fact, the president's policy was nothing less than an undeclared war against France. The nation of backwoods farmers was about to flex its muscles on the high seas.

THE CONFLICT WITH FRANCE The basic design work for the six frigates was done by the master shipbuilder Joshua Humphreys of Philadelphia. Humphreys was perhaps the greatest naval architect of his time. George Washington, who personally commissioned him to do the job in 1794, could not have picked a better person. In his proposal, Humphreys wrote to the president: "As our own navy will for a considerable time be inferior in numbers, we must consider what size ship will be most formidable."[3]

What the Navy got was six of the best frigates ever built. Larger than European frigates, they also carried more powerful guns. Their hulls were made of red cedar and live oak—two extremely durable hardwoods that grew only in North America—which gave the ships a shot-resistant coat of "armor" seventeen to twenty-two inches thick. Most of all they were fast, enabling them to outrun a superior enemy force.

The first three frigates ready for the new Navy were the *Constitution, Constellation,* and *United States.* The next two, the *President* and *Congress,* were just as well built, but for various reasons they did not achieve the eventual fame and glory of the first three. The last of the original six frigates, the *Chesapeake,* was a fine but unlucky ship, destined for infamy.

The USS Constitution *flew a full acre of sail.*

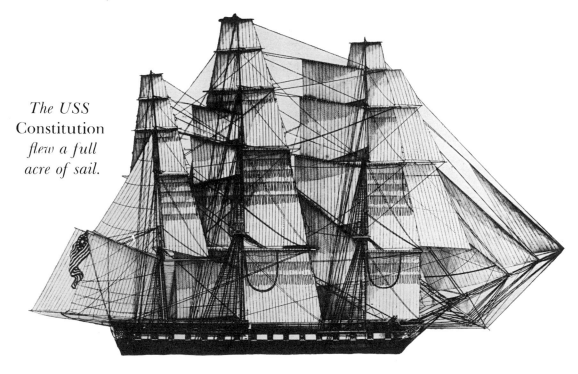

The new frigates were exactly what America needed: the best ships in their class, perfectly suited to the problem facing a tiny navy. It is no wonder Britain's greatest admiral, Horatio Nelson, would later say: "I see trouble for Britain in those big frigates from across the sea."[4]

But this was only 1798, and it was the French whom the United States was fighting. Before this conflict was over, the U.S. Navy would grow to a respectable thirty-four vessels. It would include several ships, such as the 28-gun *Boston* and 36-gun *Philadelphia*, that were built by proud and patriotic communities and donated to the Navy. In all, the U.S. Navy would capture eighty armed French vessels.

The first vessel captured was the 14-gun *Le Croyable*, taken by the 20-gun *Delaware*. (The *Delaware* was commanded by Stephen Decatur, Sr., the father of the man who would later capture the *Macedonian*.) *Le Croyable* (which, ironically, had been built in Baltimore just that year) was renamed the *Retaliation* and taken into the U.S. Navy. That fall (1798) the *Retaliation*, under the command of Lieutenant William Bainbridge (an officer who was to have more than his share of bad luck), was recaptured by the French. (She was the only U.S. Navy ship captured during the conflict with France, and the Americans had the satisfaction of taking her back from the French the following year.) The ship that took her was the dreaded *Insurgente*, a sleek and powerful 40-gun cruiser that had terrorized many an American merchant skipper.

In January 1799, the 38-gun *Constellation* caught up with the *Insurgente*. The *Constellation* pounded the French frigate from port to starboard and twice crossed the T to rake her bows with broadsides. In an hour, the *Insurgente* was reduced to a flaming hulk. Lieutenant Bainbridge was avenged.

One year later the *Constellation* came up against the mighty, 50-gun *La Vengeance*. The two ships fought a grueling five-hour duel of almost unparalleled ferocity. Three times the French captain tried to surrender his ship, but—shrouded in smoke, amid the roar of cannon fire—the Americans neither saw his flag come down nor heard his call. Riddled

The Constellation *(left) crosses the T to deliver a broadside*
to the Insurgente *during the undeclared war with France.*

with holes but still afloat, *La Vengeance* finally drifted off
into the dark Caribbean night.

On October 12, 1800, the *Boston* defeated *Le Berceau* in
the last battle of the undeclared naval war with France. Unknown to the captains of either ship, a peace convention
had already ended the hostilities between France and the
United States (no talk of bribes this time). The French would
go on to conquer most of Europe, but they'd had enough
of the new American Navy.

The American government spent about $6 million on the
Navy from 1797 to 1800. In that time the insurance rates
on American merchant ships operating in Caribbean waters
dropped by $8.5 million—a saving that was almost ten times
the cost of the six frigates. American exports grew to more
than $200 million. And federal revenue from tariffs on im-
ports rose to more than $22 million.

Signing the U.S.–French peace treaty.

Thus the naval war with France demonstrated that in a dangerous world, a strong navy could be vital to a healthy national economy. This lesson, however, was lost on the United States government. Congress voted to reduce the peacetime Navy.

A plan to build six ships of the line was scrapped. (Ships of the line were the battleships of the day, with two or three gun decks and between 60 and 120 guns.) Most of the Navy was sold. The naval officer corps was reduced to 150 midshipmen (officer apprentices), 36 lieutenants, and 9 captains. In fact, the U.S. Navy might have disappeared completely had it not been saved, ironically, by the Barbary pirates.

THE TRIPOLITAN WAR

When President Thomas Jefferson took office in March 1801, American relations with the Barbary States were approaching a new crisis. It began when the warship *George Washington,* commanded by the unlucky William Bainbridge, was sent to deliver the usual payment of tribute to the pasha of Algiers.

When the American ship entered the inner harbor of Algiers, coming under the guns of the harbor's defenses, Captain Bainbridge was bluntly informed that the *George Washington* must sail at once to Constantinople (under the Algierian flag!) to deliver a payment to the sultan of Turkey. Completely at the mercy of the harbor forts, Captain Bainbridge had no choice but to comply with this outrageous demand.

As it turned out, the visit to the Turkish capital was a diplomatic success: The American skipper was given high honors by the sultan. Nevertheless, when his ship got back to America, Captain Bainbridge delivered a furious report to the president that ended with the words: "The next time I am directed to deliver tribute, I hope it will be through the mouths of cannon!"[5]

The account of the *George Washington*'s forced mission to Turkey aroused national indignation. When the pasha of Tripoli (modern-day Libya) demanded an increase in tribute, even President Jefferson, a pacifist, was pushed too far.

Instead of tribute the president sent a squadron of U.S. warships, with orders to protect American trade. Hoping to frighten and intimidate the Americans, the pasha declared war on the United States. The war, however, was a farce. Tripolitan cruisers, brimming with ragged, fierce-looking scoundrels, still searched the waves for defenseless American merchant ships, but they strictly avoided any convoys protected by American warships.

The first two years of the war saw only one battle. It was between the little 12-gun schooner *Enterprise* and the brig *Tripoli.* (A brig was smaller than a frigate and had only two masts.) Despite its advantage in size and firepower, the Tripolitan ship was no match for the Americans' superior sail-

*Captain William Bainbridge delivering
tribute in Algiers.*

ing and marksmanship. Without losing a man, the *Enterprise* repeatedly raked the enemy's bows. The pirate ship, having lost half its crew of eighty, was forced to surrender.

In 1803, however, the situation became serious when the 36-gun *Philadelphia* was captured. Its captain, "Hard Luck Bill" Bainbridge, had lost another U.S. Navy ship, only the second one ever to be taken. Yet it wasn't really the skipper's fault. While chasing a Tripolitan cruiser, the *Philadelphia* ran aground on an uncharted reef. She heeled over sharply to one side, so that none of her guns could be brought to bear. The Tripolitan pirate barges swarmed all over the stricken American vessel. On the next high tide the pirates wrenched the ship free from the reef and towed her triumphantly into port.

Captain Bainbridge and his crew of 22 officers and 315 men were thrown into the slave pens of Tripoli. They would give the pasha bargaining power with the American government. The loss of the *Philadelphia* also meant that the American Mediterranean squadron lost about twenty percent of its firepower. Worst of all, the Tripolitan Navy had acquired its largest and most dangerous warship.

The remainder of the American force, under the command of Commodore Edward Preble, proceeded at once to block Tripoli's harbor. All through the savage winter of 1803–1804, the Americans maintained as tight a blockade as the stormy weather would permit. After studying the harbor's layout, Commodore Preble concluded that it would not be possible to capture the well-guarded *Philadelphia*. But he thought there was a chance that she might be put out of service.

Preble sent a small boat into the harbor on the night of February 16, 1804, with a hand-picked crew of eighty-four volunteers. Their mission was to board and destroy the *Philadelphia*. So as not to arouse suspicion, the boat was an old Tripolitan ketch, captured for the purpose and rechristened the *Intrepid*. The man who led this suicidal mission was the young skipper of the *Enterprise,* Lieutenant Stephen Decatur. Most of the men were concealed, along with many casks of gunpowder. Lieutenant Decatur and a few others visible on deck were dressed as Maltese sailors. At the boat's wheel was Salvatore Catalano, a Sicilian pilot enlisted as a guide. He knew every rock and shoal of the harbor and could speak Arabic.

The *Intrepid* had no guns—everything depended on the stealth and nerve of the crew. At 10 P.M. she approached the *Philadelphia.* A voice called out from the frigate, ordering the ketch to keep clear. In Arabic, Catalano said that his boat had lost her anchor and requested permission to tie up alongside the big frigate for the night. A line was passed to the ketch; but as the two vessels touched, a Tripolitan watchman suddenly cried, "Americans!"

"Board 'em!" shouted Lieutenant Decatur. The Americans scrambled up the frigate's sides, their sabers glinting in the moonlight, and hoisted each other through the gun ports. The American seamen cut down some twenty Tripolitans before the rest panicked and jumped overboard. Within fifteen minutes the ship's decks were cleared of the enemy.

The *Philadelphia* was then set afire. Lieutenant Decatur was the last man off the burning ship. He leapt into the rigging of the *Intrepid* as she pulled away. By now shots from the harbor forts were splashing around the ketch.

The blaze aboard the *Philadelphia* quickly crept up her masts and glowed through her gun ports. As the frigate's loaded cannons heated up, they began to fire. One broadside flew into the city, the other into the fort closest to the escaping Americans.

Not only did the little ketch work its way back out of the harbor with dozens of shoreside guns roaring at it, but not one crew member was lost on the mission. The news of the American exploit was an instant sensation. The great British admiral Lord Nelson called it "The most bold and daring naval act of the age."[6] Congress voted American citizenship for the Sicilian Catalano. President Jefferson rewarded the twenty-five-year-old Decatur with a full captain's commission.

The pasha was furious. He demanded that the Americans *pay him* for the loss of the *Philadelphia*! On hearing this, the normally dour Preble laughed aloud. He became convinced that force, not tribute, was the key to making the Barbary States respect the American flag. The burning of the *Philadelphia* was to be just the beginning of the pasha's troubles.

As fair weather returned to the Mediterranean, Commodore Preble made plans to lead his whole squadron into the heavily defended port. This was unheard of. According to naval doctrine, wooden ships had little chance against thick-walled stone harbor forts. Pitting inches of oak against yards of masonry was lunacy. There would also be the Tripolitan Navy—twenty armed barges and brigs—to deal with.

Yet Preble had confidence in his men and great contempt for the accuracy of the Tripolitan gunners. He was also aided by the king of Naples, who loaned him six small gunboats and two mortar boats (each of which carried one large, high-angled gun designed to hurl bombs over walls).

On August 3, 1804, the Americans sailed into Tripoli. The 44-gun *Constitution* led the way, pouring out broadsides hot and fast. At the height of the battle, nine Tripolitan gunboats converged on three of the borrowed Italian gunboats, which were manned by Americans led by Stephen Decatur. The Tripolitans intended to board and fight hand to hand, but the outnumbered Americans did the boarding. The Barbary pirates were said to be invincible in hand-to-hand combat at sea. In the two hours of fierce fighting that followed, the Americans completely shattered that myth. They captured three of the Tripolitan gunboats and drove off the other six. From that day on the Tripolitans refused to engage the Americans in close action.

At one point a Tripolitan captain had pretended to surrender his vessel to Lieutenant James Decatur, Stephen Decatur's younger brother. But as the American officer stepped on board to take possession of the boat, the Tripolitan captain shot him in the head. Word soon reached Captain Stephen Decatur that his younger brother had been killed by treachery. In a fury he found the enemy gunboat, grabbed a long pike, and led his men in boarding.

Finding the enemy captain who killed his brother, Decatur lunged at him with his pike. The Tripolitan captain, however, wrested the pike from Decatur and turned its needle-sharp point against him. Decatur drew his sword, but its blade was broken off at the hilt by a heavy blow from the burly Tripolitan's pike. The now-defenseless American sprang at his opponent, clutching the enemy captain's throat with his bare hands.

The two men fell together and rolled on the deck. The Tripolitan drew a dagger, but not before Decatur reached the pistol in his jacket. He blocked the dagger blow with his left hand and squeezed the trigger with his right, firing through his own pocket. The Tripolitan crumpled, and Decatur stepped free.

The new U.S. Navy was tested at Tripoli on August 3, 1804.

Stephen Decatur struggles with a Tripolitan pirate in hand-to-hand combat at the Battle of Tripoli.

Over the next month the American squadron bombarded Tripoli repeatedly. While the Americans were making rubble of the city and its forts, it is said that the pasha took shelter in his deepest dungeon and that his fortress gunners had to be driven to their posts with whips.

Throughout the fall and winter a tight blockade of the port was maintained and plans were made to renew the bombardments the following summer. Meanwhile, William Eaton, a former Revolutionary War captain turned soldier of fortune, was organizing a force of Tripolitan rebels in Egypt. With the help of some U.S. Navy ships, he captured the port city of Derna on April 27, 1805. Of the handful of Americans who took part in the assault, seven were U.S. Marines. (The second phrase of the Marine Hymn commemorates their action on the "shores of Tripoli.") They lowered the Tripolitan flag and hoisted the Stars and Stripes in its place. It was the first time the American flag flew over an Old World stronghold.

The pasha, fearing further bombardments and now trembling for his throne, agreed to release the American captives if the U.S. Navy would go away. In June a treaty, without tribute, was signed.

There were two lessons for the world to learn from the Tripolitan War and the undeclared war with France: first, that there was a limit to how far the United States could be pushed around; and second, that a young nation can be very sensitive when it comes to the rights and safety of its citizens. Sadly, the British were about to demonstrate that they had not learned these lessons very well.

CHAPTER 4

THE SECOND WAR OF INDEPENDENCE

While the U.S. Navy was punishing the pasha of Tripoli, the French Empire was steadily pushing its boundaries across the map of Europe. Only Britain resisted completely. And Britain's needs in its long fight with France would eventually contribute to war with the United States. The British believed strongly that in fighting Napoleon, they were fighting for freedom against tyranny. Yet the longer the war with France went on, the more they suppressed freedom in their own country and violated the rights of neutral countries such as the United States.

Britain's fleet was its lifeblood. Yet in view of the conditions aboard British warships, keeping the 150,000-man Royal Navy fully crewed with able-bodied British seamen was no easy task. Life aboard a British warship was dirty, dreary, and dull. It was hard work, too. Sailors were constantly hauling on ropes, mending sails, and scrubbing decks.

The food was not only bad, it could be deadly. Meat, when available, was preserved only by layers of salt. It was always old, usually rotten, and certainly covered with purple-black mold. The hard-as-rock navy biscuits were home to an assortment of creatures. Sailors would tap the biscuits on the table before eating them to shake some of the maggots, mites, and beetles out of their burrows. Some men would eat in dark corners so as not to see the putrid food they shoved into their mouths or the slimy green water they flushed it down with.

Worst of all was the cruel discipline of the Royal Navy. Seamen were lashed on the bare back with a cat-o'-nine-tails for almost any offense. Serious offenses, such as being disrespectful to an officer, carried penalties of hundreds of lashes, an ordeal that killed or crippled many men. Floggings were usually a daily occurrence. On many ships the last man out of his hammock in the morning was whipped until he bled.

The backbreaking work, poor food, and harsh discipline caused thousands of men to desert the Royal Navy. Because of this, British naval captains seldom granted shore leave, adding to the misery of navy life. It was not uncommon for British seamen to go three years without setting foot on land. For many, the only hope was that an opportunity to escape might present itself.

Deserters usually fled to America. Many even became U.S. citizens. A lot of them signed up on American merchant ships. Service aboard those vessels was more relaxed and much easier than in the British Navy, and the pay was about ten times higher.

Under British law, if a British warship was undermanned, its captain had the right to stop any British merchant ship on the high seas and impress the vessel's "excess crewmen" into his own crew. The Navy captain would send a press gang aboard to take off the strongest and most skilled sailors. The merchant captain was sometimes left with less than half his crew after a visit from the Royal Navy.

By 1805, British Navy captains were routinely stopping American merchant ships as well. They claimed that they were searching for deserters, but this was used as an excuse for impressment.

Britain considered any Englishman aboard an American vessel to be a deserter. But how do you tell an Englishman from an American? At this time, most American families had originally come from the British Isles. Even as late as the early 1800s, both peoples looked and sounded pretty much the same. Backed by a squad of Royal Marines, a British officer could call anyone he wanted a deserter. It's not surprising that many American citizens were "mistaken" for deserters.

Even when the British found a real deserter, he may have become an American citizen. Britain, however, recognized no form of naturalization. It considered any former British subject to still be one, and that included anyone born in America before 1776. The press gangs operated on the principle: "Once an Englishman always an Englishman."[7] That was more than just a saying; it was a rule enforced by the guns of British warships.

The American government vigorously protested this as a lawless violation of the rights of its citizens. The British, however, felt that the Americans were selfishly putting their sense of national pride above Britain's wartime needs. After all, the war Britain was waging against France was on behalf of mankind. The British held that their right to use any means available to continue their noble fight to defend the "free" world outweighed the rights of a few American seamen.

THE ORDERS-IN-COUNCIL

In 1805, four months after the end of the Tripolitan War, the British fleet under Lord Nelson defeated the French fleet off Cape Trafalgar in the greatest naval battle of the nineteenth century. The Battle of Trafalgar all but eliminated the French Navy, and with it any French hopes of invading the British Isles.

After Trafalgar, Napoleon turned all his energies eastward. An amazing string of victories gave the French Empire control of continental Europe. By 1807 only Britain was still at war with France. The world's most powerful navy faced the world's most powerful army—and that brought fighting to a stalemate.

Since they could not fight directly, Britain and France tried to get at each other economically. Britain issued a series of decrees called Orders-in-Council, proclaiming blockades of Napoleon's Europe. Most important, Britain declared that neutral ships trading with Europe would be liable to capture by the Royal Navy unless they first called at a British port to pay a fee and obtain a certificate. Napoleon, in return, announced that any neutral vessel that paid the fee or even allowed itself to be searched by a British warship would be subject to seizure at any port on the European mainland.

The United States, the world's largest neutral carrier, was caught in an economic cross fire. It was nearly impossible to carry on trade without violating the guidelines of one side or the other. Yet, while Napoleon's decrees were deeply resented by the Americans, Britain's Orders-in-Council were despised. One reason was that Britain enforced its decree by stationing warships right outside U.S. ports.

The Royal Navy, although huge, did not have enough ships to blockade the hundreds of miles of Europe's coastline. Thus the Orders-in-Council authorized British captains to search any American merchant ships on the high seas that were thought to be headed for a "blockaded" port. However, catching a sleek Yankee trading ship on the open ocean was not so simple. It was easier to wait outside harbors and stop the U.S. ships as they came and went. Thus every major American seaport soon was shadowed by British warships. Few merchant ships moved through their entrances without being stopped and searched for French-made goods or contraband (smuggled goods) bound for Europe.

In principle, the United States government actually acknowledged Britain's right to stop and search vessels suspected of carrying contraband. But the United States believed the search should consist of examining the ship's papers. The British, however, combed the ships from bow to stern.

Worst of all were the impressments of American sailors that often accompanied these searches. Americans considered both the searches and the impressments a clear violation of the sovereignty of the United States. They recalled the ominous words of Benjamin Franklin: "The War of the Revolution has been won, but the War of Independence is still to be fought."[8]

American sailors dreaded impressment. There were stories of men who jumped overboard and drowned rather than face a life of hell aboard a British warship. One American sailor, who was told to go below deck and pack his duffel bag, chopped off his left hand so as not to be taken. And yet, between 1805 and 1812, over 6,000 Americans (more than the number of seamen in the U.S. Navy) were impressed.

One way for a seaman to protect himself against impressment was to sign up on an American warship. This option appealed naturally to a good number of Royal Navy deserters, who might get caught on an American merchant ship. The pay in the U.S. Navy, while not as good as in the merchant service, was higher than that in any regular navy in the world.

The former British seamen found life in the U.S. Navy very strict and orderly, as it was in the Royal Navy. Yet the American officers were fair and reasonable men. The meals, while not fancy, were good, stick-to-your-ribs fare. Most of all, the men were treated like human beings. Physical punishment was very rare on American warships, and even serious offenses carried a maximum penalty of twelve lashes.

THE CHESAPEAKE-LEOPARD AFFAIR

The presence of a British deserter on a U.S. Navy ship sparked an incident that brought the United States and Britain close to war early in 1807. On January 22, the frigate *Chesapeake* sailed out of Hampton Roads, Virginia, bound for the Mediterranean to join the American squadron still patrolling there. The ship was expected to be overseas for at least two years and was loaded with supplies. The war in Europe made it difficult to get supplies and materials there. What could be gotten was usually of low quality and expensive. The more supplies the *Chesapeake* could bring with her, the better.

The ship's decks, therefore, were piled high with extra coils of rope, bolts of sailcloth, barrels of flour, boxes of biscuits, kegs of beer, chicken coops, spare timbers, and duffel bags. Somewhere under all this clutter (but no one was sure exactly where) were the black powder horns and slow-burning match cord that were needed to prime and fire her 36 cannons.

By 2 P.M. the Virginia coastline was fading into the western horizon. On the eastern horizon a fair blue summer sky met the calm sea. With good weather the *Chesapeake* would reach the Mediterranean in five or six weeks. Her skipper, Captain James Barron, was expecting a pleasant and routine transatlantic voyage. Destiny, however, had other plans for this American warship.

Among the crew was a man who enlisted under the name Wilson, but evidence suggests that his real name was Radford or Ratford. He was a deserter from the Royal Navy who had defected to the United States and joined the U.S. Navy. Several weeks earlier he had been on shore leave in Norfolk when a visiting British naval officer recognized him on the street. The affair might never have come to anything had Radford not publicly insulted the officer.

It seems that Captain Barron knew about the incident but did not think it was a very serious matter. The worst he could imagine was a diplomatic protest by the British minister in Washington. The *Chesapeake* was a fully recognized major warship of the U.S. Navy. He knew there was nothing more the British could do about it.

"Sail ho!" yelled the lookout. Approaching the *Chesapeake* was the 50-gun British frigate *Leopard*. About an hour later, the two ships were within speaking distance.

"I have a message for you," shouted the captain of the *Leopard*. "Request you heave to and receive my boat."[9]

The *Chesapeake* furled her sails, coming to an almost complete stop. The *Leopard* lowered a rowboat with a British officer who in a few minutes was aboard the American ship.

In the captain's cabin, the British lieutenant presented Captain Barron with a written request that the crew of the *Chesapeake* be mustered on the main deck and questioned to find out if any of them had deserted from the Royal Navy. (The captain of the *Leopard* was, in fact, well aware that Radford was on board.) Stunned by this unprecedented request, Captain Barron sent the lieutenant back with a message that under no circumstances could the captain of a national vessel of the United States permit the inspection of his crew by officers of a foreign nation.

Why Barron did not immediately give the order for battle stations is a mystery, for the *Leopard* had already opened her gun ports. When the lieutenant was back aboard the British warship, he reported everything that he had seen to his captain. He emphasized the unready state of the *Chesapeake*'s gun deck.

As the *Leopard* closed in, Captain Barron at last ordered battle stations. But waiting for the *Chesapeake* to get organized was not in the British captain's plan.

"Sir," shouted the British captain, "I have orders to remove British deserters from your ship! Heave to or I shall fire!" No response came from the *Chesapeake*.[10]

Turmoil gripped the gun deck of the hapless American ship. So much cargo lay around the guns that they were difficult to get at. Even worse, the match cords could not be found. Without her guns the *Chesapeake* was a toothless shark.

In the midst of the feverish attempt to find the firing equipment, there was a thunderous crash. The *Leopard* had unleashed a full broadside at point-blank range! Cannonballs smashed into the hull, sending up a hailstorm of splinters. Yet the *Chesapeake*'s guns were silent. Never had an American warship been more unprepared.

"Return fire!" shouted Captain Barron, as if his order could miraculously take the place of combat readiness and preparation. A second broadside crashed into the *Chesa-*

peake. Flying splinters tore into the captain's leg. He staggered, steadied himself on a wooden post, and shouted in a voice choking with emotion: "Open fire! My god, will no one do his duty?"[11]

A third broadside crashed aboard, then a fourth and a fifth. Below deck the shrieks of the dying mingled with the groans of the wounded and the enraged curses of others.

Had this been a regular battle, the damage so far would be considered no more than might be expected. The enemy, supposedly, would have been hurt also. Under these tragic circumstances, however, it was pure horror. The confusion was now beyond remedy. The *Chesapeake* was a sitting duck.

Finally a lone American gun fired a single shot. A young lieutenant had grabbed a red-hot coal from the galley in his bare hands, rushed to the gun, and slammed the searing coal down to fire the cannon. It was the only gun fired by the *Chesapeake* during the entire miserable action, in which twenty-one Americans were killed or wounded. The *Leopard* replied with her sixth broadside.

Captain Barron gave the order to strike the colors. Down fluttered Old Glory. The same British lieutenant returned, this time with a squad of Royal Marines. He lined up the crew for inspection.

The terror-stricken Radford hid below but was found. He was rowed over to the *Leopard* and promptly hanged from the topmast for desertion and resistance—crimes compounded by his insult to an officer of the Royal Navy.

In addition, the lieutenant identified three more men—a black man, an Indian, and a white man from Maryland—as having deserted from the ship of the line *Melampus*. The three men had in fact deserted from the *Melampus*, but they were American citizens, born in America and impressed into the Royal Navy from an America merchant ship. They had simply escaped their captivity, but they were now enslaved again.

James Barron was court-martialed and found "guilty of neglecting, on the probability of an engagement, to clear

British officers removing sailors from the USS Chesapeake.

his ship for action." He was sentenced to five years' suspension from the Navy. Captain Stephen Decatur was a member of the board of inquiry, despite his request to be excused. (Decatur and Barron had been midshipmen together on the *United States* during the naval war with France and were good friends.) Years later Barron fought a duel with Decatur over the matter and shot him dead. (As his second—the go-between who arranges the details of a duel—Decatur chose unlucky William Bainbridge.)

After the *Chesapeake* was repaired and refitted, Captain Decatur was given the task of whipping her crew into fighting shape and restoring their morale. He rigorously drilled his gun crews and repeatedly assured them that if a British warship so much as looked funny at their ship, the *Chesapeake* would repay the blood insult she had received.

For two years Captain Decatur looked for, but never saw, the *Leopard* on the horizon. One can only guess what would have happened had he gotten his wish.

THE EMBARGO ACT

In the wake of the *Chesapeake-Leopard* affair, war fever broke out in all parts of the country. Americans were outraged—they demanded war with Britain to avenge this affront to the American flag.

"Never since the Battle of Lexington," said President Jefferson, "have I seen the country in such a state of exasperation."[12] Yet the thought of the further bloodshed and destruction that a war would bring was hideous to the president. He knew there must be a peaceful alternative.

President Thomas Jefferson hoped to avoid war with Britain.

In response to the incident, Jefferson launched one of the boldest experiments in the history of American foreign policy.

Instead of war, Jefferson believed that Britain could be brought to terms by means of economic pressure. The European war had reached a stalemate and had become a contest of mutual economic strangulation. As Britain's number one trading partner, the United States occupied a delicate position in the balance of power.

On the recommendation of the president, Congress passed the Embargo Act of 1807, halting all trade with the whole world. No American vessels were permitted to sail on the high seas (Jefferson's solution to the impressment problem). No European ships could bring their goods to American seaports. It was hoped that the Embargo Act would convince Britain to revoke its Orders-in-Council and Napoleon his corresponding decrees.

For Napoleon, however, the Embargo Act was a windfall. It deprived British manufacturers of their largest and most profitable market, and it denied British colonies much-needed American goods and services. Only by declaring war with Britain could the United States have helped France more.

In addition, Jefferson's timing could not have been worse. Less than a year later, Napoleon conquered Spain, which set in motion the disintegration of its vast overseas empire. American merchants had been waiting years for South American markets to open up. Just when Spain's monopoly over its colonial trade had finally been broken, the embargo prevented American merchants from taking advantage.

Thus, British merchants were able to take over a lion's share of the lucrative South American trade. This greatly reduced damaging shortages caused by the embargo. In the long run, the Embargo Act was no more than a severe inconvenience for Britain, not the powerful tool of economic pressure President Jefferson had hoped for.

The worst irony of the embargo was that it nearly ruined the American economy. While hundreds of ships lay idle at their docks, thousands of men who made their living on the sea were out of work. In New England, businesses went bankrupt, banks folded, and people lost their life savings. In the South, many planters were ruined as the price of cotton fell fifty percent. The one part of the country that actually benefited was along the Canadian border, where a thriving smuggling trade arose.

The embargo also caused government revenue to dwindle. Trying to make ends meet, Congress reduced the regular Army to 3,500 men. Military cuts came right at the time when the United States was moving into a period of crisis in its foreign affairs. Even more remarkable, the Navy was also starved for funds during a time of maritime troubles.

At last President Jefferson was forced to admit his policy had failed. Just before leaving office in March 1809, he signed a bill to repeal the Embargo Act. It was replaced by the Non-Intercourse Act, which allowed Americans to trade with all nations except France and Britain. The British continued to search ships and impress American sailors.

TOWARD WAR

In the congressional election of 1810, nearly half the seats went to new members. Among them was a group of energetic congressmen who became known as the War Hawks. They denounced what they considered the do-nothing policies of the former Congress and felt it was time for a bold new approach to foreign policy. As most of the War Hawks were from the southern and western states, their main concern was with the Indian threat.

The War Hawks were especially worried about Tecumseh, chief of the Shawnees. Tecumseh had been born near present-day Dayton, Ohio, and his father had been killed by settlers. Although only a child, he fought for the British during the Revolution. Tecumseh, whose name means "Panther-lying-in-wait," believed that the Indians could block the westward expansion of the white settlers by putting to rest old tribal quarrels and banding together. He dreamed of a united Indian nation stretching from the Great Lakes to the Gulf of Mexico.

Each year Tecumseh traveled thousands of miles to preach his message to the scattered Indian tribes. Nowhere was the new spirit of unity stronger than in a town he built along the Tippecanoe Creek in northern Indiana. In this, Tecumseh's "capital," Shawnees, Wyandottes, Ojibwas, Kickapoos, Delawares, and Ottawas lived together as brothers.

Fearful of Tecumseh's growing strength, the settlers decided to act before it was too late. In 1811 the governor of Indiana Territory, William Henry Harrison, organized a thousand-man force and advanced along the Tippecanoe.

Tecumseh was away visiting southern tribes and wasn't expected back for several months. He had left his brother, a medicine man named the Prophet, in charge, with instructions not to fight until he returned. If the Americans did come, the Prophet was to promise them anything to avoid a battle.

The Prophet, however, believed his magical powers would help him defeat the Americans. He told the braves that a spell would make the white man's bullets as soft as raindrops. On November 7, 1811, he led them in an attack on Harrison's camp. He learned, at terrible cost, that his magic charms were no match for military discipline and firepower. The Americans shot down hundreds of tribesmen and burned their capital to the ground.

The Battle of Tippecanoe won Harrison the fame and prestige that would one day help him become president of the United States. The more immediate effect of the battle was that the British now formed an alliance with Tecumseh. From his base in Canada, Tecumseh raided the American Northwest frontier and bided his time, waiting for the big war he believed was coming soon.

The War Hawks—led by congressmen such as John C. Calhoun of South Carolina, whose mother had been scalped by Cherokees, and Felix Grundy of Tennessee, who had lost three brothers in Indian raids—raised fury over Brit-

The Battle of Tippecanoe, in 1811.

ain's open assistance to Tecumseh and his followers. They clamored for war with Britain and an immediate invasion of Canada.

The War Hawks believed that so long as Canada was a British colony, the Indians would always have a power base. Most War Hawks favored American occupation of key border areas, rather than an outright annexation of the whole of Canada. Some, however, held the belief that Canada was destined to become part of the United States. They claimed it was the duty of Americans to "liberate" the Canadians, who would surely welcome them with open arms.

Even some of the congressmen who were not War Hawks thought that Canada should be conquered, but not with the idea of keeping it. Rather, they thought Canada could be held as a "hostage" to make Britain cooperate on the more important issue of "free trade and sailors' rights."

Surprisingly, the representatives of the New England states, where people had suffered most from Britain's high-handedness at sea, were strongly opposed to war with Britain. The reason was that they knew that the British would immediately blockade American seaports. Fresh on their minds was the havoc wreaked on the New England economy by the Embargo Act. The despised embargo had lasted only fifteen months; there was no telling how long a war might drag on.

Finally, on June 1, 1812, President James Madison delivered an address before a joint session of Congress. In it he reviewed British-American relations since 1803 and cited the main grievances. First was impressment, the oldest wrong. Next were the British ships hovering near American ports, harassing U.S. shipping, and the Orders-in-Council, which suppressed free trade and violated America's neutral rights. Finally, Madison raised the issue of the renewed Indian warfare on the Northwest frontier.

On June 4, the House of Representatives voted 79 to 49 to declare war. But ironically, as the Senate was preparing to debate the declaration, the British were reassessing their policies toward the United States. America's four-year-long boycott was finally producing economic distress in England. Exports to the United States had dried up, and badly needed food imports from America were down to a trickle.

An English crop failure the previous fall had been followed by a bitter winter. Starved and jobless, English workers had staged riots, while merchants and manufacturers begged Parliament to revoke the Orders-in-Council and re-open American trade. That spring the British prime minister was assassinated (a rare event in British history) by a disgruntled worker. Britain finally decided on June 16 to revoke the unpopular Orders-in-Council.

But this news would take weeks to reach America, and by the time it did it was too late. On June 17, by a vote of 19 to 13, the Senate passed the declaration. When the president signed it the next day—June 18, 1812—the United States was at war with Britain.

President James Madison.

CHAPTER 5

INVADING CANADA

The news of the declaration of war drew mixed reactions from the American public. Southerners and Westerners cheered the declaration, while New Englanders jeered it. Yankees contemptuously called the conflict "Mr. Madison's War." A Massachusetts congressman who had voted for the war was kicked about the streets of Plymouth by angry townspeople.

Meanwhile, military planners were hastily drawing up plans for the invasion of Canada. There could not have been a better moment to strike. The British Army was almost totally committed to the war against Napoleon on the Spanish Peninsula. It had few troops to spare for Canada, and these were not top-quality soldiers. In all, fewer than 5,000 British regulars were there, supported by about 3,000 reliable Canadian militia. With this small force, Canada's governor-general, Sir George Prevost, had to defend 1,700 miles of open border with the United States.

Luckily for Prevost, the incredibly overconfident Americans were unbelievably unprepared. There were less than 7,000 men in the regular Army, and they were strung out along forts from Maine to Georgia and Detroit to New Orleans. Yet the War Hawks still seemed to think that taking Canada was just a matter of marching.

Military planners were counting heavily on the various state militias, about 35,000 men in all. They clung to the fantasy of minutemen, America's noble citizen-soldiers, springing bravely to arms to defend the homeland. The reality was that despite a proud tradition, militia units had often proved to be unreliable during the Revolution and played only a limited role in winning that war.

Moreover, it was apparent from the start that the governors of the New England states would stand on their constitutional right to use their militias only for self-defense. A militia unit could not be forced even to leave its home state, let alone go out of the country.

This meant that there would not be a large pool of militia available to support a thrust from the Northeast, the only area where a decisive blow could be achieved. Even when militiamen were available, they were a poorly armed, undisciplined rabble for the most part. Their training consisted of gathering on the village green a few times a year to march around a little and fire their muskets in the air before settling down to a picnic in the shade.

By contrast, soldiers in the regular Army were as good as any in North America. Yet the same could not be said of the generals. There were a total of seven, all of whom had served the country well during the Revolution but were now in their sixties and had not led soldiers in battle for thirty years.

The plan for the invasion was simple enough. Three forces would strike across the Northeast border from New York State (at Fort Niagara, Sackett's Harbor, and Plattsburg), then link up and capture Montreal, the key to Canada's defense. About the same time, a fourth force would move out from Detroit and take Fort Malden on Lake Erie.

THE FALL OF THE NORTHWEST

The commander of the Detroit operation was General William Hull. The red-faced, sixty-year-old Hull was described at the time as "a short, corpulent, good-natured

THE WAR IN THE NORTH (1812)

old gentleman who bore the marks of good eating and drinking."[13] Hull admitted that he was unfit to command and asked to be replaced, but President Madison persuaded him to take the job.

By July 5, General Hull was ready to move out with about 1,200 militia and 800 regulars. Yet he was already losing confidence in the plan. About 800 civilians, including his own daughter and grandchildren, lived in Detroit, and another 4,000 or so civilians in the surrounding area. He began to worry about their safety. While General Hull hesitated, his men grew disgusted with his lack of nerve and constant delays.

Finally, on July 12, Hull led his men across the Detroit River into Canada. But his progress was painfully slow. At last he ordered the attack on Fort Malden to begin, but he changed his mind the next day. He had received word that Fort Michilimackinac, a key American outpost at the juncture of Lake Michigan and Lake Huron, had fallen to a British and Indian force. Tortured by the thought of bloodthirsty Indians flooding into Michigan Territory, Hull panicked and ordered his troops back to Detroit.

A few days later, two men met at Fort Malden who, as commanders, were exactly the opposite of General Hull. Both men were bold, energetic, and ambitious. Both inspired confidence in their men and won their devotion. They shook hands, a handshake that would soon spell disaster for Hull.

On one end of this handshake was Tecumseh, chief of the Shawnees. On the other end was General Isaac Brock, commander of the British forces in western Canada.

General Brock's superior was Sir George Prevost, who believed that all British forces should remain on the defensive. Brock, however, believed that now was the time to strike in the West. Brock also knew that his Indian allies might lose faith in the British unless he quickly took them on the offensive.

Brock now proposed to Tecumseh that they attack Detroit at once. Delighted, Tecumseh immediately drew his hunting knife and carved a map of the area on a roll of birch bark. On August 15, General Brock crossed the Detroit River into Michigan Territory and began to prepare an assault on the American positions.

Brock had only about three hundred British regulars, along with about four hundred Canadian militia and Tecumseh's six hundred warriors. He was up against more than 2,000 American defenders in well-prepared strong points. To reach them, Brock's men would have to march across an open field commanded by heavy American artillery. (These cannons, incidentally, were originally captured from the British at the Battle of Saratoga in 1777.)

It is doubtful that the British would have been able to take Detroit by brute force. General Brock, however, was a master of psychological warfare, and the weak-willed General Hull was the perfect victim. One trick Brock used was to dress his militiamen in scarlet coats to make the Americans think that they were up against a large force of British regulars.

Brock's best weapon was General Hull himself. Several of Hull's letters had been intercepted by the British. They not only betrayed the low morale of the American troops, but more important, they expressed the American commander's fear of Indian massacres. Brock now did all he could to exaggerate the Indian threat, preying on Hull's anxiety.

As the sun began to set, Tecumseh's braves swam the Detroit River. They emerged from the water on the American shore like creatures from another planet. Their bodies, naked except for moccasins and a loincloth, were painted with bizarre patterns and colors. Their hair was spiked up with bear grease. Scalping knives, held between their teeth, flickered in the fading light.

That night Hull lay awake to the sound of an unnerving multitude of coyote howls and the crows of wild turkeys as the Indians "talked" to each other. Much worse, Brock had arranged to have one of his messengers captured by the Americans with a document saying that the British had 5,000 Indian warriors with them.

By morning General Hull's nerves were completely shot. A broken man, he couldn't even raise his eyes to look at his officers. He sat on the ground with his back against a dirt rampart, paralyzed with fear, and shoved chewing tobacco into his mouth until a dribble of brownish yellow spittle ran down his chin and onto his chest.

As Brock's men advanced cautiously across the open field, the American gunners waited anxiously for the order to open fire. Hull just sat there. He was tormented by a summons from Brock to surrender. It ended by saying that if the British were forced to take Detroit by storm, they could not answer for the conduct of the Indians toward the townspeople.

As the minutes ticked by, some officers decided that the time had come to mutiny. They intended to arrest the general, take command, and give the order to shoot. But by the time they were ready to act, they were too late. Hull had already brought down the colors and run up a white sheet in the flag's place.

The American militiamen were sent home after taking an oath not to fight again for the rest of the war. (Although this practice seems strange today, it was not uncommon then.) The regulars and their officers were sent to a prisoner-of-war camp in Canada. Later in the war, General Hull was exchanged for some British prisoners and court-martialed for cowardice. He was sentenced to be hanged, but kindhearted President Madison pardoned him.

General Hull surrendering Detroit to General Brock.

For all that Hull worried, the civilians at Detroit were not mistreated by the Indians. This was due to the presence of the honorable Tecumseh. He ordered his braves, under penalty of death, not to torture, murder, rape, or steal from the civilians.

White settlers were not always so fortunate. When General Hull had learned about the fall of Fort Michilimackinac in August, he feared an Indian attack on Fort Dearborn (the site of present-day Chicago). He had sent Captain William Wells with orders to evacuate the post.

The small garrison there told Captain Wells that they would rather take their chances in the fort than run the risk of getting caught in the open. In spite of this, and a warning from a friendly Pottawattami chief named Black Partridge that leaving the fort would be suicide, Wells was determined to carry out his orders. On the morning of August 15 (the day before the surrender of Detroit), the soldiers and their families abandoned Fort Dearborn and headed south along the shore of Lake Michigan.

Five hundred Indians ambushed the column along a stretch of sand dunes about a mile from the fort. Over half the Americans were killed and scalped, including twelve children. The rest were taken prisoner and held for ransom. The warriors beheaded Captain Wells, then carved his heart out and ate it.

THE MONTREAL CAMPAIGN

The disasters at Fort Michilimackinac, Fort Dearborn, and Detroit meant that Michigan Territory was lost and were probably the worst news of 1812. But things went no better in the Northeast. Expecting that the Americans' next attack would be on the New York–Canadian border along the Niagara River, General Brock hurried back to his headquarters there at Fort George.

When he arrived, he was astounded to learn that a truce had been arranged! When General Prevost had learned that his government had revoked the Orders-in-Council, he had sent a message to the American commander in the Northeast, General Henry Dearborn, informing him that there was no longer a reason for the Americans to fight a war. (Dearborn had fought at Bunker Hill in the Revolution, but now, at sixty-one, he was too fat to even mount a horse and had to lead his men from a buckboard.)

"Granny" Dearborn, as his men called the silver-haired general, had told Prevost that he did not have the authority to declare a cease-fire, but he would order all American forces to go on the defensive. Obviously, when both sides go on the defensive there is no fighting.

Not only did the truce stall the American offensive until the beginning of October, it also gave Prevost and Brock time to strengthen their defenses along the border. When President Madison found out that nothing was happening in the Northeast, he angrily rejected Dearborn's agreement with Prevost and ordered the general to resume hostilities at once.

As Brock had predicted, the American blow came from Fort Niagara. Brock had only about 1,600 soldiers and 300 Indians to defend the forty-mile Niagara frontier. The Americans had at least 6,000 men, but only a fourth were regulars. The rest were undisciplined militia, mainly from New York and Pennsylvania.

The Americans decided to start by taking the high ground overlooking the village of Queenston, seven miles below the falls. The first attempt, on the morning of October 11, 1812, failed when the first assault boat was rowed across the Niagara River with all the oars for the other boats stacked in it. The following night the Americans tried again.

About two hundred troops had made it across the river when they were spotted around 4 A.M. by a British sentry, who sounded the alarm. In the skirmish that followed, the British were pushed back to Queenston. Awakened by the distant thunder of cannon fire, General Brock at Fort George assembled his forces and marched toward the battle.

When Brock got there, he found the Americans had already captured Queenston Heights. By 2 P.M. about seven hundred or eight hundred American troops were firmly

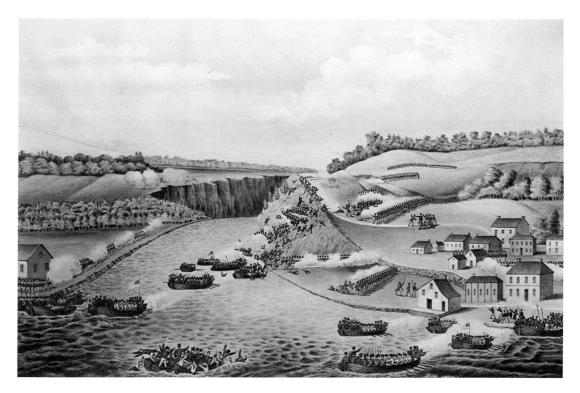

The U.S. assault on Queenston Heights was successful, but the Americans could not hold the position.

established atop the heights. They were commanded by a towering twenty-six-year-old officer named Lieutenant Colonel Winfield Scott (who would go on to great fame in the Mexican War). The American victory would be complete as soon as the rest of their troops crossed the river.

The militiamen, however, had no stomach for the reality of combat. The sight of the wounded returning from battle caused the semi-trained, part-time soldiers to lose their nerve. Their commanding officer rode up and down the ranks pleading with them to act like men and enter the waiting boats, but none did. The militia just stood by shamefully and watched the British rally to attack their countrymen across the river.

Abandoned by the militia, Colonel Scott and his men fought the brave but hopeless Battle of Queenston Heights.

Many Americans who were not killed or wounded tried to swim the swift Niagara only to drown in the attempt. Most of the others were forced to surrender, including Scott.

The British had won an important victory, but at a terrible price. While charging up the face of the heights at the head of a company of British regulars, General Brock was shot in the chest at close range and killed. Not only did the Canadians lose a great patriot, they now had to fight the rest of the war deprived of their best military strategist.

The third prong of the invasion schedule, the attack from Sackett's Harbor, New York, was not even attempted. The fourth prong, moving up Lake Champlain from Plattsburg, was led personally by General Dearborn with between 6,000 and 8,000 men.

On the night of November 19, a detachment of U.S. regulars crossed the border, fought a short skirmish, and captured a blockhouse. The Canadian defenders then slipped away into the darkness while the confused Americans got lost in the woods and fired on one another. Again the militia refused to leave the country. Frustrated and disgusted, Dearborn sent the militiamen home and marched the Army into winter quarters at Plattsburg.

With this, the land campaign of the first year of the war came to an end. Those five months of almost slapstick folly on the Canadian border represent one of the bleakest chapters in American military history.

In fairness, not all the blame rests on the bungling American generals. Although inept and incompetent for the most part, they were also severely hampered by a remarkably inefficient military system. This was the consequence of past policies of pacifism and penny-pinching that had practically disarmed the country.

Throughout the war, the Army's faulty supply organization would cause shortages of essential materials, equipment, ammunition, and rations. The food was notoriously bad at times. Purchased by the federal government from the lowest bidder, it sometimes was uneatable.

(The character "Uncle Sam" originated in 1812. It started with an Army meat inspector named Samuel Wilson, from Troy, New York. He would stamp boxes and barrels of contracted salted meats with a large "U.S." Supply workmen told the troops in jest that the initials stood for "Uncle Sam" Wilson. Soon the nickname was applied to any government-supplied item, and it later came to mean the federal government itself.)

Although the invasion effort for 1812 ended with disgrace at Detroit, tragedy on the Niagara, inaction at Sackett's Harbor, and a fizzle from Plattsburg, all was not gloom. National honor was to some extent redeemed that year by a notable string of American naval victories on the high seas.

CHAPTER 6

FIGHTING ON THE HIGH SEAS

While maritime troubles with Britain were coming to a head back in the spring of 1812, the Department of the Navy had had plenty of time to carefully formulate a detailed strategy for the best use of the American fleet. Amazingly, when the government declared war in June, no such plan existed.

One reason for this was that few people in Washington believed that America's tiny fleet could do anything more than sit out the war in port, acting as floating gun batteries for the harbors. Apart from a couple of hundred thinly spread little gunboats assigned to protect numerous bays, lakes, rivers, inlets, sounds, and other inland and coastal waterways, the U.S. Navy consisted of sixteen "blue water" (oceangoing) vessels.

By contrast, the Royal Navy consisted of 1,048 ships, including 116 frigates and 120 mighty ships of the line. Altogether Britain's huge fleet mounted over 28,000 guns and was crewed by 150,000 seamen. The U.S. Navy could put to sea just over 400 guns and fewer than 5,000 seamen.

Moreover, Britain's fleet was considered invincible. In the previous fourteen years of nearly continuous warfare, the Royal Navy had lost only five out of more than four hundred battles fought against European navies. In all five cases, one or more small British vessels were trapped by a much larger enemy force. Never had a lone British warship ever been beaten by a single enemy ship of the same class.

If the Navy Department was intimidated by the size and record of Britain's venerable Navy, American naval captains were not. They believed that their ships were as good as or better than any in the Royal Navy and hungered for the chance to prove the mettle of themselves, their crews, and their vessels. Appalled by the notion of having their fine frigates spend the war rotting in port, several naval officers, led by Stephen Decatur, persuaded Washington to send the Navy into action. They argued that the fleet could be of great use in the war effort by disrupting British maritime trade—England's lifeblood—and intercepting enemy supply ships.

Thus the U.S. Navy set off under orders to scour the sealanes in search of British merchant vessels, avoiding contact with British warships when possible. As the Royal Navy began closing a ring around American waters, however, clashes with U.S. fighting ships became inevitable.

OLD IRONSIDES It was about 3 P.M. on August 19, 1812, when the 38-gun British frigate *Guerrière* and the 44-gun *Constitution* spotted each other on the horizon, about 750 miles east of Boston. At that hour and that distance either one could have escaped the other. Instead, the two warships went straight toward each other like two medieval knights charging, lances level. Each was bent on defending its country's honor.

At 5:00 P.M. the *Guerrière* turned sideways and began firing prematurely (the British captain was hoping to finish the battle before dinnertime) while the American ship continued to maneuver just out of range. The American skipper, a boisterous and daring sea dog named Captain Isaac

Hull (the nephew of General William Hull), continued to jockey for position until his vessel was precisely where he wanted it.

When the wind was directly behind his ship, Hull spread full sail and knifed straight for the enemy. The *Constitution*'s towering masts held more than an acre of canvas to catch every breath of the breeze.

Taken aback by the American frigate's swift and sudden movement, the *Guerrière* fired several disorganized and ineffectual broadsides. A few of the shots that hit merely bounced off the *Constitution*'s thick oak hull. A Yankee seaman cried out, "Her sides are made of iron." From that day forward the ship was known as "Old Ironsides."

The Constitution *defeating the* Guerrière.

Soon, however, the *Constitution* drew into close range, and even her "iron" sides could not stop some enemy cannonballs from piercing through her hull. The American gunners began to wonder how long their captain was going to wait before giving the order to shoot.

Captain Hull intended to hold fire until the moment it would have the greatest physical, and psychological, impact. As the American frigate sliced through the water at lightning speed, the enemy's fire quickly grew louder and more intense. Hull waited.

The American gunners, standing by helplessly while their comrades fell dead or wounded around them, wondered if their captain had gone mad. Hull still waited.

The *Constitution* continued to bear down on the British ship, and the *Guerrière* kept on pounding it without response. Finally, when the *Constitution* was only fifty yards away—half pistol range—Hull gave the order to fire as only an American captain would: "Now, boys, pour it into them!"[14]

Every gun on the port side of the *Constitution* fired simultaneously in what seemed like a single explosion. The concussion from the ear-splitting blast sent a shock wave through the American ship that rattled men's teeth and vibrated their bones.

Slammed with 736 pounds of hot metal at point-blank range, the gun deck of the *Guerrière* suffered a moment of unimaginable horror. Flying splinters shredded men's flesh. One man was impaled on the opposite side of the ship by a huge chunk of jagged timber that drove through his chest. Others were torn up by ricocheting hunks of sharp-edged shrapnel. A few were even directly hit by cannonballs.

The crew of the *Guerrière* was completely shaken and disordered, precisely the effect Captain Hull was counting on. Before the enemy crewmen could regroup themselves, a second thunderous broadside crashed into them. Again a hurricane of iron and shattered wood swept through the *Guerrière*'s gun deck.

While the *Guerrière* became a floating slaughterhouse, the

Constitution cut across the British ship's bow to cross the T. The American gunners then proceeded to dismantle the *Guerrière*'s rigging. First, the mizzenmast became the mizzen stump; then the foremast fell; finally, the mainmast teetered gently as if it were about to faint, then plopped into the sea. Realizing the futility of further resistance, the *Guerrière* surrendered, the first British frigate to strike her flag to an American warship.

The *Guerrière* was sinking. She could not be salvaged. After her crew was taken aboard, the *Constitution* sailed back to port. When the ship reached Boston, Captain Hull learned the painful news that his uncle had surrendered Detroit.

Not only did Isaac Hull's victory redeem the family name, it gave the public a sorely needed reason to celebrate. As one historian put it: "The shattered hulk of the *Guerrière*, which the nephew left at the bottom of the Atlantic Ocean, 800 miles east of Boston, was worth for the moment the whole [territory] which the uncle had lost, 800 miles to the west."[15]

October brought more good news for the country to celebrate. On the 18th, the 18-gun American sloop of war *Wasp* engaged in a grueling, close-in gun duel with the 20-gun *Frolic* east of Chesapeake Bay. When the two ships collided, an American boarding party, led by a former impressed seaman, hacked its way across the enemy's decks to win the day. And on the 25th, the *United States* pummeled the British frigate *Macedonian*, which was brought back and taken into the U.S. Navy.

With more dismal reports coming from the Canadian front, the news of naval victories did wonders for public morale. If the victories were good for the people, they were even better for the president, who was facing a tough election in November. By using the good news from the war at sea to downplay the disheartening news from the war on land, Madison was able to save his political career.

The next major naval engagement came four days after Christmas, when the *Constitution*, while cruising for British merchant ships off the coast of Brazil, was approached by

John Bull stung to agony by the Wasp and Hornet.

the 38-gun *Java*. The captain who had defeated the *Guerrière*, Isaac Hull, had by now been promoted to commander of the Boston Navy Yard. Old Ironsides' new skipper was "Hard Luck Bill" Bainbridge.

William Bainbridge was a competent and able naval officer, but misfortune seemed to haunt his career. He had lost the *Retaliation* during the naval war with France and, later, the *Philadelphia,* for which he had to spend almost two years in a Tripolitan dungeon. He had also been the one who was forced to sail the *George Washington* to Turkey under the flag of Algiers. More than a few men aboard the *Constitution* feared for the worst as their luckless skipper drew their ship into battle.

The seesawing hit-and-run contest that followed was a naval fencing match that pitted the skill and cunning of each captain against the other. The *Java* was definitely the faster ship. Old Ironsides, however, was probably more maneuverable—that is, until she had the bad luck of having her wheel torn away by a British cannonball. Debris from the wheel flew into Captain Bainbridge's leg. The captain, however, coped remarkably well with both his pain and the near-fatal disadvantage of having to steer his ship by shouting orders through a hole in the deck to the seamen who operated the rudder manually with a makeshift arrangement of cables.

In the end, the *Constitution*'s good star proved to be more powerful than Bainbridge's bad luck. Mast by mast, Old Ironsides dismantled *Java*'s rigging until the British frigate was a helpless hulk rolling on the waves. Too mauled to repair, the *Java* had to be blown up, sending yet another British warship to the bottom of the ocean.

Impressive as they were, America's naval triumphs amounted to pricking a whale with a pin. Their military significance was almost nil. They did little to alter the reality of Britain's naval supremacy on the high seas. Yet these victories were critical to the war effort. The U.S. Navy had managed to restore the American people's confidence in their military establishment. Without this, the public might have lost hope and collapsed into pessimism and despair.

The psychological effect on the British public was also considerable. The reaction of the English people to the news of the defeat of the *Guerrière* was one of shock and disbelief. *The Times* of London called it "too painful to dwell upon." [16]

The public mood turned to outrage when the news of the *Macedonian* arrived. "What is wrong with British seapower?" [17] asked *The Times*. Then came the *Java*. With shame and gloom, *The Times* printed this article:

The public will learn that a third British frigate has struck to an American. . . . Upward of 500 British [merchant] vessels [have also been] captured in seven months by the Americans. . . . Can these statements be true? . . . Anyone who would have predicted such a result of an American war this time last year would have been treated as a madman or traitor. He would have been told that the American flag would have been swept from the seas [and] the contemptible navy of the United States annihilated . . . yet down to this moment not a single American frigate has struck her flag.[18]

Alas, that was soon to change.

"DON'T GIVE UP THE SHIP" In February 1813, the 18-gun *Hornet,* under the command of Captain James Lawrence, won a brilliant victory over the 18-gun *Peacock,* sinking the British brig in twelve minutes. As a reward, Lawrence was given a frigate to command. He arrived in Boston on May 20 to take charge of his new ship, the 36-gun *Chesapeake.*

The *Chesapeake* was one of the original six frigates, but she was the runt of the litter. The best sailors and equipment always went to her five big sisters. On the day she was launched, the *Chesapeake* got stuck while sliding down the ways and twice had to be pried loose. It was an inauspicious beginning to an ill-fated career.

After the *Chesapeake*'s unfortunate encounter with the *Leopard,* Stephen Decatur had turned the ship's crew into an efficient, synchronized, well-oiled fighting machine. But when Decatur took command of the *United States* in 1809, he took his finely sharpened crew with him. After that it was always difficult for the Navy to find good sailors who were willing to sign aboard the *Chesapeake.* The crew that Captain Lawrence inherited in May 1813 was a disorganized lot of superstitious, semi-trained seamen.

The two critical factors in every American naval victory had been better seamanship and teamwork. Captain Lawrence, however, had only nine days to get the *Chesapeake* ready to sail. There was not enough time for him to master the sailing qualities of his new ship or to make his crew an efficient fighting team.

And battle was waiting right outside the harbor. After the sinking of the *Java,* the British Admiralty had issued orders forbidding its frigate captains to engage any of the

American "superfrigates" in a one-on-one fight. Yet the commander of the 38-gun British frigate *Shannon*, Captain Philip Broke, felt that the time had come to debunk the myth of American invincibility in single-ship combat. He had studied U.S. naval policy for years, with particular attention to its emphasis on gunnery tactics and training. He had also learned from the mistakes of the British captains who had met disaster at the hands of the Americans.

For a month Captain Broke drilled the *Shannon*'s crew to perfection with one purpose in mind—to tackle the *Chesapeake*. When the American frigate sailed out of Boston harbor on June 1, 1813, he was lying in wait for her like a tiger. The *Shannon* and her crew were ready, as ready as a ship could be.

The battle went pretty much the way Broke and his men had rehearsed it. During the fight Captain Lawrence was mortally wounded. His dying words would become the motto of the U.S. Navy: "Don't give up the ship!" Refusing to surrender, the *Chesapeake* was finally boarded by a wave of eager British marines and sailors. Only then was Old Glory hauled down, by the British.

For the United States, the loss of the *Chesapeake* was a terrible blow that could have been avoided if she had only been handled the way her construction and design had deserved.* Yet she had not gone down without a fight. The battle was the bloodiest naval engagement of the war. Only later, in 1814, aboard the *Essex,* would more Americans be killed in a naval action. Aboard the British ship, more men were killed or wounded than on any other victorious ship on either side. The number of British seamen killed was actually greater than that of the beaten frigates *Guerrière, Macedonian,* or *Java.*

*After being repaired the *Chesapeake* became part of the British fleet. In 1820 she was finally broken up. Her fine timbers were used to build a flour mill in Wickham, England, where they can be seen today. The *Shannon* seems to have been damaged beyond economical repair. In any case, she was retired from the Royal Navy shortly after the battle.

*The death of Captain Lawrence, from an 1860
painting. His last words—"Don't give up
the ship!"—became the Navy's rallying cry.*

Badly wounded in the battle, Philip Broke retired from the service. For his admirable triumph he was made Sir Philip Broke, baronet. He had showed that it was possible to beat the American superfrigates (the littlest one, anyway) in a one-on-one fight. The British Admiralty, however, learned a different moral from the *Chesapeake-Shannon* story. After that, British frigates sailed only in pairs or as part of a squadron.

THE CRUISE OF THE *ESSEX*

Despite its early victories, the U.S. Navy's fighting days were numbered. Half its ships were already captured or bottled up in port by blockading British ships. As the war in Europe went steadily better for Britain, more British warships were sent to American waters.

The last single-ship battle of the war took place on September 5, 1813, off the coast of Maine, between the U.S. schooner *Enterprise* and the British brig *Boxer*. After a hard-fought battle during which both captains were killed, the American ship emerged the victor. By the end of the year, however, only two U.S. Navy vessels, the *Constitution* and the 32-gun light frigate *Essex,* were still at sea.

The story of the *Essex* merits telling. It had begun a year earlier, in December 1812. The ship had been prowling in the South Atlantic when her adventurous skipper, Captain David Porter, decided it was time for a bold move.

Acting on his own initiative, Porter sailed his ship around Cape Horn, into the Pacific, making the *Essex* the first U.S. warship ever to enter that ocean. For the next year he proceeded to totally destroy the British Empire's whaling fleet in the South Pacific. Each captured ship gave the *Essex* all the quantities of food, water, medicine, tar, paint, rope, and sailcloth she needed to remain at sea.

To give his men a well-earned rest, Porter anchored the *Essex* for seven weeks at the very remote island of Nukahiva, 2,500 miles southeast of Hawaii. As would be expected of sailors who had been at sea for a year, the Americans became quite friendly with some of the natives. On leaving that paradise, Captain Porter claimed Nukahiva for the United States and renamed it Madison's Island.

Meanwhile, the Royal Navy was closing in. None too pleased by the loss of their whaling fleet, the British had dispatched extra warships to the area to search for the Americans. On March 27, 1814, a British squadron finally caught up with the *Essex* off the coast of Chile, after she lost her main topmast in a heavy squall. Trapped, Porter put up a gallant but hopeless defense. Battered to splinters, the *Essex* struck her flag. And that was the end, for the time being, of American sea power in the Pacific.

THE BLOCKADE Meanwhile, in the Atlantic, Britain's grip on the eastern seaboard had tightened. Despite the enormous expense of keeping a huge blockade fleet on station twenty-four hours a day, the British believed that the havoc it would wreak on the American economy justified the cost.

Indeed it did. Once-thriving import and export industries went bankrupt. Import duties—a prime source of government revenue—dried up. The blockade also disrupted coastal transportation. The alternative way to move goods was by land, along America's limited network of largely unmaintained dirt roads. This method was painfully slow and very expensive. For example, a hundred-pound sack of Carolina rice sold for about $3 in Charleston. By the time that sack reached Philadelphia it cost $12. The cost to transport a $9 barrel of Louisiana sugar from New Orleans to New York was over $30.

A blockade, however, can be a two-way street. The loss of foodstuffs and raw materials from America caused shortages in Britain and in Spain, where the British Army was campaigning. In fact, it soon proved almost impossible to keep the troops in Spain supplied without American goods.

Fortunately for the British Army, there were many New Englanders with anti-war sentiments who were willing to help. The Royal Navy turned a blind eye as clandestine commerce flowed from New England. For Americans to be trading with the enemy was not only illegal, it was treason. Yet the lucrative underground trade with the British continued throughout the war.

In order to keep its blockade ships provisioned, the Royal Navy resorted to plundering American coastal communities from Cape Cod to Georgia. British sailors and marines would simply go ashore whenever they pleased, raiding pantries, pigsties, and chicken coops. One British captain even sent his men to harvest potatoes for the ship's mess.

The worst raids by far were carried out by a cold-blooded Yankee-hater named Admiral Sir George Cockburn. His squadron marauded up and down Chesapeake Bay, pillaging the countryside and terrorizing the populace. When the people of Havre de Grace, Maryland, tried to resist one of Admiral Cockburn's pirate raids, he burned forty of the sixty homes that made up the town. After driving off the local militia at Hampton, Virginia, Cockburn's men looted houses, raped several women, and killed an old man in bed.

THE AMERICAN PRIVATEERS

By the end of April 1814, the *Constitution* was finally bottled up in port. Yet even with the whole U.S. Navy under lock and key, the war at sea was far from over. The task of destroying British commerce now passed to the privateers.

Privateers were privately owned merchant vessels converted into mini-warships. Before such a ship could sail, she would have to obtain a privateer's license from the government. This ensured that if she were captured, her crew would be treated as prisoners of war. Without a license they would be promptly hung for piracy.

For the British, blockading the main ports and bays was one thing, but sealing off every inlet, river, creek, cove, and island along America's jagged 1,500-mile coastline was impossible. Privateers could easily hide out in waters too shallow for deep-draft warships until darkness, fog, or foul weather came to cover their escape. Once they were out on the open sea, the fleet, sleek American privateers could outrun almost any ship in the Royal Navy.

The waters of the West Indies were the favorite hunting ground of the American privateers, but some operated as far away as the North Sea and Indian Ocean. Many privateersmen came from the crews of blockaded U.S. Navy ships. Not surprisingly, at least three privateers were christened the *Decatur*.

Not all privateers restricted their activities to commercial targets. A number of them routinely attacked military transports bound for Spain, creating a shortage of food, ammunition, and equipment for the British troops fighting there. One cavalry regiment had to campaign on foot after an American privateer captured the boat carrying their horses. Thus, while some Americans treasonously sent supplies to the British Army, others dutifully took them back.

The careers of individual privateers and the daring exploits of their captains have filled books. One privateer captured a town in Scotland; another held an island off the British coast for a week. A Baltimore privateer almost single-handedly ruined Britain's West Indian sugar trade.

The king of the privateersmen was Captain Thomas Boyle. Once, while he was stalking in the English Channel, Boyle issued a proclamation to the people of London declaring the British Isles to be "in a state of strict and rigorous blockade."[19] When the Royal Navy finally flushed him out of the Channel, Captain Boyle fled to Cuba, capturing a 20-gun British warship along the way.

Boyle's blockade proclamation was meant as a joke to mock the Royal Navy, but there was some truth to it. The American privateers caused prices in England on mercantile goods to skyrocket. Sugar, coffee, cocoa, and citrus fruits became luxuries of the wealthy.

Although there were no more than fifty American privateers prowling at any one time, the damage they inflicted was a constant drain on Britain. Not only did the British lose many valuable ships and cargoes, but the cost of insuring them soared out of reach. In all, the privateers captured or destroyed 1,345 vessels. The fact that in the closing months of the war the British were losing an average of two ships a day did much to help bring about peace.

Yet long before the last battles were fought at sea, many more had been fought on land. When, in December 1812, the U.S. Army marched into winter quarters following the fiasco on the Canadian border, the War of 1812 had only just begun.

CHAPTER 7

THE STRUGGLE FOR THE NORTHWEST

Americans were deeply troubled by the loss of Michigan Territory. Regaining control of the Northwest frontier became the government's top priority. The general picked for the job was William Henry Harrison, who had defeated the Shawnees at Tippecanoe in 1811. In the winter of 1812–1813, the thirty-nine-year-old general built a fortified camp near the mouth of the Maumee River, about sixty miles south of Detroit. He named it Fort Meigs in honor of the governor of Ohio. There he waited for reinforcements and for spring.

A thousand-man reinforcement column of Kentucky volunteers, under Brigadier General James Winchester, was on its way to Fort Meigs in January 1813 when it received a distress message from Frenchtown (later Monroe, Michigan), a small American settlement on the River Raisin. The town was reported to be occupied by only 150 Canadian militia and Indians.

General Winchester and his men marched immediately to the rescue. Getting there was a tortuous ordeal through two feet of snow and subzero temperatures. On January 17, 1813, the shivering, half-starved Kentuckians reached Frenchtown. After a brief skirmish the enemy was driven off, leaving behind large quantities of valuable supplies.

THE RIVER RAISIN MASSACRE

Why General Winchester decided to hold Frenchtown is still a mystery. With General Harrison's main body of troops too far away to help, the British, only twenty miles away in Detroit, were almost sure to strike back. Yet Winchester not only remained in a clearly overextended location but also set up the worst possible defensive position and neglected to post advanced sentries.

Five days later a superior British and Indian force pounced on the virtually unfortified American position. Within minutes, one hundred men were scalped and General Winchester was captured as the American right flank collapsed. On the left flank, however, the Americans under Major George Madison fought fiercely, repulsing British charges again and again.

When a British officer appeared waving a white flag, Madison's men cheered, thinking the enemy was surrendering. Actually, the officer was bringing a message from the captive General Winchester, saying that he had surrendered on behalf of the entire army. Major Madison, however, refused to capitulate unless the British promised that they would provide for the care and safety of all American prisoners and protect the wounded from the Indians.

The British commander was a scoundrel named Colonel Henry Proctor. He had replaced General Brock, after Brock was killed at Queenston Heights. Proctor was also left in charge of the Indians until the return of Tecumseh, who was away drumming up support among the southern tribes.

At first Proctor refused to grant any conditions for surrender. Major Madison replied that in that case he and his Kentuckians intended to fight to the last man. Having lost many troops on these stubborn Americans and not wanting an already costly fight to drag on, Proctor promised to give the prisoners the best possible treatment.

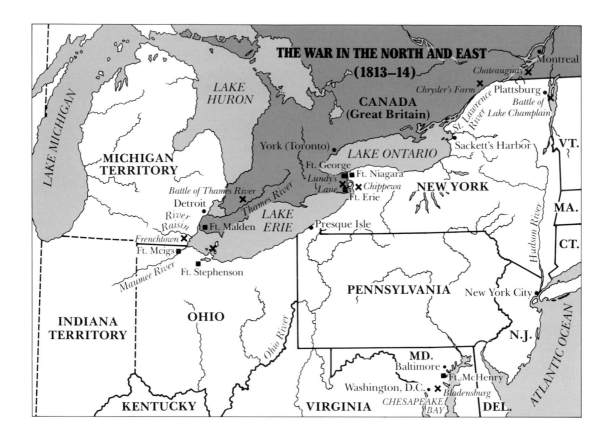

The War in the North and East (1813–14)

The unscrupulous British commander did not keep his word. As soon as the Americans laid down their weapons, they were stripped of their warm coats and forced to drag supply sleds back to Detroit so that the British could rest their horses. The wounded prisoners were left behind unguarded.

That night the Indians began scalping the wounded. (The scalps were sent to Colonel Proctor at Fort Malden as trophies.) One house with a number of prisoners was set afire. As the wounded tried to crawl out the doors and windows, the Indians pushed them back into the flames. "Remember the River Raisin" soon became the rallying cry of the Northwestern army.

General Harrison hoped to pay back the British in the spring, when all the reinforcements had arrived, but he knew that there was little his army could do while the British controlled Lake Erie. Although the enemy had only six small gunships, that was six more than the Americans had. So long as the British Lake Erie flotilla was unopposed, there was little chance of retaking Detroit because the British could quickly send supplies and reinforcements by water. They could also land troops behind the advancing Americans and cut their line of supply at will. Congress had, in fact, already authorized and funded the building of a Lake Erie flotilla at Presque Isle (now Erie, Pennsylvania), but it would be many months before it was ready.

THE SACKING OF YORK

To the east, on Lake Ontario, the British and American flotillas were about equal in strength. By the spring of 1813, however, the British had nearly finished building the *Sir Isaac Brock,* a 30-gun frigate (a huge ship by Great Lakes standards), at York (present-day Toronto), the capital of Upper Canada.

Knowing that this powerful new ship would tip the scales against them, the Americans staged an amphibious raid at York on April 27. They landed a 1,600-man brigade, commanded by Brigadier General Zebulon Pike (the famous soldier and explorer for whom Pikes Peak was named). The American forces drove off the Canadian garrison, captured the harbor's shore batteries, and burned the *Sir Isaac Brock.*

The Americans would have left without further incident had not a large store of gunpowder blown up at a captured battery. The explosion killed or wounded over two hundred Americans—including General Pike, who was crushed to death by a falling stone. Although the Canadians themselves suffered about sixty casualties, the Americans angrily accused them of treachery. The soldiers retaliated by looting a number of vacant houses. Later, they burned government buildings when some scalps were found inside one of the legislative meeting halls.

The sacking of York and the destruction of the government buildings left the British with deep feelings of ill will toward the Americans. Before this war was over, they swore to repay the insult.

The death of
General Pike at York.

Throughout the summer, the fighting in the Northeast seesawed indecisively. The Americans captured Fort George on the Niagara but were thrown back at the Battle of Stony Creek. The British dealt a humiliating blow to the Americans at the Battle of Beaver Dams but completely botched up an operation against Sackett's Harbor.

In the fall, the American Army made a second attempt to take Montreal. It ended with the disastrous defeats at the battles of Chateauguay and Chrysler's Farm. In December, the British easily recaptured Fort George (the American militia had gone home for the holidays), and the year ended with both sides back where they started.

"WE HAVE MET THE ENEMY AND THEY ARE OURS"
Back in the Northwest, General Harrison was still gathering supplies at Fort Meigs and trying to replace the men lost at River Raisin. Hoping to crush Harrison before he could be reinforced, Colonel Proctor and Tecumseh had attacked Fort Meigs in May. After an unsuccessful eight-day siege, the British gave up the attempt.

[82]

The British did, however, manage to cut off some of Harrison's reinforcements on May 5, when a column of Kentuckians walked into a trap. About six hundred Americans were killed or captured. Again the Indians began to scalp and massacre the prisoners. One courageous British regular was murdered when he tried to protect the Americans. Colonel Proctor, however, did nothing to restrain the warriors. The situation had begun to look like River Raisin all over again when Tecumseh, on horseback, came charging down on his bloodthirsty men like an avenging angel, whacking them on the head with the flat side of his sword.

After he cowed his braves, Tecumseh rode over to Proctor and shouted at him with rage, "Begone! You are unfit to command. I conquer to save, and you to murder."[20]

Tecumseh defending American prisoners.

On July 20, the British again laid siege to Fort Meigs. Again they failed. Anxious to win at least a small victory for his efforts, Colonel Proctor withdrew his force on July 29 and attacked Fort Stephenson three days later. The fort, located on the Sandusky River about twenty-five miles east of Fort Meigs, was defended by only 160 soldiers. When Harrison sent orders to evacuate the fort, the able and resourceful twenty-three-year-old commandant, Major George Croghan, replied, "We have determined to maintain this place, and by heaven, we will."[21]

By heaven, they did. Major Croghan and his handful of Kentucky riflemen held off Colonel Proctor's 1,400-man force. Each time the British charged the fort, they were mowed down by Croghan's sharpshooters and his one artillery piece, called "Old Betsy" by the men, which belched repeated muzzle-loads of nails and buckshot. By Proctor's own account, "The fort, from which the severest fire I ever saw was maintained, was well defended."[22]

The British packed up and went back to Fort Malden. Little did they know that the next time they had to face the business end of those deadly Kentucky rifles, it would be in Canada.

Meanwhile, work was proceeding on the U.S. Lake Erie gunboat flotilla. A small army of shipwrights, carpenters, and laborers toiled many long months under the tireless, painstaking supervision of the stubborn and energetic twenty-seven-year-old naval officer who was to command the mini-fleet.

That man was Master Commandant Oliver Hazard Perry (not to be confused with Matthew Perry, his younger brother, whose famous mission forty years later would open trade with Japan). By mid-August 1813, Perry was ready for action. He sailed his flotilla of nine combat vessels to Sandusky Bay for a conference with General Harrison. The two men discussed plans for the reconquest of the Northwest.

After Harrison lent him some "marines" (one hundred buckskin-clad Kentucky sharpshooters) to round out the

*Oliver Hazard Perry was a lieutenant when
he took command of the Lake Erie fleet.*

fleet's fighting strength, Perry sailed off to start putting the squeeze on the British. Ranging the lake, Perry's gunboats brought enemy traffic to a halt. Proctor (now a general) was faced with a critical supply pinch at Fort Malden. He sent his fleet out to find and destroy the Americans.

The two flotillas met at Put-in-Bay in the western end of Lake Erie on September 10, 1813. The British force consisted of two ship sloops, the 19-gun *Detroit* and 17-gun *Queen Charlotte*, two small brigs with 13 and 10 guns, and two single-gun boats. The Americans had two 20-gun brigs, a schooner of 4 guns, and six boats mounting 1 to 3 guns each.

Although the firepower on each side was about equal, the Americans had more stubby, powerful carronades but many fewer long-range guns. Perry knew that he had to get close enough to use his short-range smashers or his brigs would be gradually chopped to bits by British long guns.

The American fleet sailed toward the British line, with Perry in the lead aboard his flagship the *Lawrence* (named in honor of Captain James Lawrence, Perry's close friend, who had been killed aboard the *Chesapeake*). Perry now unfurled his battle flag, which he had been saving for this day. It was a nine-square-foot piece of blue cloth embroidered with seventeen white letters: DON'T GIVE UP THE SHIP.

The *Lawrence* took many hits before she reached the enemy, and a number of her guns were knocked out. In essence, the ship "took the heat" so that the rest of Perry's boats could close in with less damage. Yet for reasons still unclear, the 20-gun *Niagara* and five other boats stood back instead of coming to Perry's assistance.

The British ships now formed a semi-circle around the *Lawrence* and the two gunboats with her. For two hours the British hammered Perry's flagship with murderous broadsides. The Americans dealt out some of their own punishment as well. Not only did the stubby carronades take their toll, but the Kentucky marines, high in the *Lawrence*'s rigging, almost wiped clean the *Detroit*'s top deck. Still, the British eventually pounded the *Lawrence* into a defenseless hulk.

The crew of the *Lawrence* displayed remarkable determination in the face of an overwhelming foe, and there were many acts of heroism. They also suffered the highest casualty ratio of any ship in the war; 83 of the 103-man crew were killed or wounded. Although he had innumerable close calls, including two musket balls through his hat, Perry was unscathed.

The *Lawrence* fought on, even when it had only one gun left. When that was knocked out, Perry did an extraordinary thing. Instead of surrendering, he pulled down his DON'T GIVE UP THE SHIP banner, slung it over his shoulder, jumped into the ship's only undamaged rowboat with four oarsmen, and made for the *Niagara*. The little boat was drenched as fountainlike splashes of cannonballs rose all around it and musket fire dimpled the water.

The British were astonished to see the rowboat reach the *Niagara*. A minute later they were stunned to see the blue and white battle flag with Captain Lawrence's famous words run up the mast. Taking command, Perry drove the *Niagara* headlong into the British center.

His ship disabled, Perry rowed to the Niagara *to continue the fight.*

As the *Queen Charlotte* turned to get the best broadside angle, one of the *Niagara*'s cannonballs snapped a rope holding the British ship's topsail in place. The *Queen Charlotte* instantly swung into the *Detroit*. As their riggings tangled into one another, the two ships became hopelessly locked together.

Seizing the moment, Perry swerved to cross the T. The *Niagara* poured a fiery hailstorm of iron into the befouled British ships. The *Niagara* then swung alongside the *Queen Charlotte* and fired well-placed shots at such close range that they tore through that ship and into the *Detroit*.

The two riddled British ships surrendered while Perry's other boats rounded up the rest of the British squadron. Perry was now master of Lake Erie.

(Perry would receive much praise for his great victory, but he was always quick to give credit to the brave and skillful seamen under his command. It is worth noting that black Americans played a major role. About a fourth of Perry's four hundred men were free blacks. Their courage led Perry to remark, "The color of a man's skin is no more an indication of his worth than the cut and trimmings of his coat."[23])

Back at Fort Meigs, General Harrison had all he could do to keep his volunteers, restless from inaction, from marching home in frustration when a messenger approached him with Perry's battle report. The note, scribbled on the back of a crumpled old envelope, reported modestly:

General. We have met the enemy and they are ours—two ships, two brigs, one schooner and one sloop. O. H. Perry[24]

At Fort Malden, General Proctor also received a report. He knew the defeat at the Battle of Lake Erie was the signal Harrison was waiting for to spring into action. Proctor made plans to evacuate his now unstable position as soon as possible and retreat to eastern Canada.

The Americans, however, were fast on his heels. Harrison sent mounted men by road to Detroit while Perry ferried the infantry to the Canadian shore four miles below Fort Malden. The Americans met only token resistance from

Proctor's rear guard as they hotly pursued the enemy. Harrison finally caught up with the main body of the British force on October 5, 1813, along the Thames River.

"REMEMBER THE RIVER RAISIN" General Proctor was well aware that much of Harrison's force consisted of Kentucky volunteers eager to avenge the River Raisin Massacre. He had no intention of being captured. As the battle began, the cowardly Proctor rode off in his carriage, leaving his soldiers behind to buy time with their lives for his escape.

The British force deployed with British soldiers formin the right flank and Indians, under Tecumseh, forming a line on the left flank. When a bugle sounded, the Americans charged, screaming "Remember the River Raisin!" and engaged in severe hand-to-hand combat. The British line buckled, then broke, from the shock of the American onslaught. On the right, the battle was over in about ten minutes. On the left, the Indians, with Tecumseh in the thick of the fighting, made a tougher stand. But musket balls finally felled the great Shawnee chief. The Indians lost hope and scattered into the surrounding swamps.

The death of Tecumseh at Thames River.

So ended the battle. Thirty-three dead braves were counted on the battlefield, along with twenty-five fallen Americans. Another fifty or so Americans were wounded. The British had thirty-five casualties, and about six hundred were taken prisoner. (Only one British officer, with about fifty regulars, escaped.)

The Battle of Thames River had several important results (not to mention the capture of about a million dollars worth of military supplies). It ended forever Tecumseh's dream of a united Indian confederation. Not only did his death effectively eliminate the political, social, and military cohesion of the Northwest Indians, but soon afterward the very fabric of the Shawnee nation began to disintegrate, never to recover.

The Battle of Thames River also marked a key point in the war. It gave the United States control of western Canada and secured the Northwest once and for all. With Lake Erie now an American pond, the British could no longer strike through America's back door. The victory also helped make up for the Army's poor performance in the Northeast and gave the disheartened American public some good news to celebrate.

The war in the Northwest was over. The United States had won. There the British had been hurled off American soil, never to return. In the East, however, the conflict was just starting to heat up. To most Americans, the war was still a distant affair. But it was about to hit home.

CHAPTER 8

BRITAIN STRIKES BACK

What was probably the most significant development of the war took place in the spring of 1814. It was not in Canada or New York, not on the Great Lakes or at sea, but in France. In April, Napoleon I, emperor of the French, surrendered his army and his throne, bringing to an end nearly twenty years of almost continuous warfare in Europe. Napoleon's downfall also brought to an end Britain's need to restrict trade, blockade continental Europe, and impress American seamen—three things that had been the core of the conflict with the United States.

Yet, if many Americans now felt that there was no longer any cause to continue the war, many Britons felt differently. The British felt that the United States had stabbed them at their greatest hour of need, while Britain struggled to free Europe from French tyranny. The time had come to turn westward and punish their ungrateful former colonies. The defeat of the French Empire meant that British Army troops stationed in Europe were now available for duty in North America. Some 15,000 battle-hardened British veterans began shipping immediately for Canada.

Meanwhile, the Americans launched another invasion on the Niagara frontier, in hope of making at least some dent in Canada while there was still time. The campaign began well, with the capture of Fort Erie (at the mouth of the Niagara) and a stunning American victory at the Battle of Chippewa a few miles to the north.

By the end of July, however, British troops were arriving in Canada in ever-increasing numbers. The scales had tipped against the Americans. After an exhausting standoff at the Battle of Lundy's Lane—the bloodiest yet fought—the American Army retreated, blew up Fort Erie, and re-crossed the Niagara into New York.

The British now prepared to launch a three-pronged invasion of the United States, which, if successful, would bring a quick end to the war on Britain's terms. The plan called for a large amphibious force to strike along the densely populated Chesapeake Bay area, to bring "hard war" to the Americans. At the same time, the main invasion force would come down Lake Champlain and follow the Hudson River to New York City, thus cutting New England off from the rest of the country. Finally, a force would be sent to capture New Orleans—which, at the mouth of the Mississippi, was the key to the West.

THE BURNING OF THE CAPITAL

In August 1814, a fleet of two dozen powerful British warships and twenty troop transports entered Chesapeake Bay. The fleet was commanded by Vice Admiral Alexander Cochrane; second in command was the dreaded Cockburn, raider of the Chesapeake coast. On board the transports were about 4,000 seasoned veterans under the command of Major General Robert Ross. On August 19, the British landed near Benedict, Maryland, thirty miles southeast of Washington, D.C.

As the British advanced, the Americans hastily prepared to make a stand at Bladensburg, Maryland, on the Washington Road seven miles from the capital. Although much larger than the British, the American force consisted mainly of green militia. On August 24, when the two forces met, the raw American troops proved no match for the polished, professional, and highly disciplined redcoats and were quickly routed.

While the Americans (including President Madison, who was at the battle) retreated in haste, the British regrouped and continued on to Washington unopposed. The capital soon became a ghost town as its citizens fled the city in panic.

Among the last to leave the city was Dolley Madison, the president's wife. Friends begged her to flee, but she was determined to save some of her husband's government documents. At the risk of being trapped by the advancing redcoats, the first lady stayed behind, stuffing her personal trunks with as many Cabinet papers as they could hold.

The showpiece of the White House was a life-size portrait of George Washington. Mrs. Madison had promised Washington's grandson, George W. Curtis, just before he left to fight at Bladensburg, that the painting would not fall into British hands. That would be an unthinkable disgrace. It had to be saved or destroyed.

Tightly screwed to the wall, the portrait could not be moved. Finally the frame was broken up with an ax, and the canvas was removed and rolled up. At last Mrs. Madison entered her waiting carriage, escaping just as the British marched into the deserted city.

Admiral Cockburn, who accompanied General Ross into the city, had long dreamed of putting Washington to the torch. Ross resisted him, preferring instead to ransom back the city to the Americans. Sadly, Ross found no Americans around to bargain with; so Cockburn got his way.

Cockburn gave the order to burn the Navy Yard, the War Office, the Treasury Building, and the office of a newspaper that had printed an unfavorable article about him. Worst of all, he ordered the destruction of the Capitol, the pride of the new nation and symbol of American independence. Years of laborious craftsmanship went up in smoke—along with law books, secret documents, veterans' pension records, and many other important papers, some dating from the Revolution.

British forces at Washington, D.C.

Next the British went to the White House, where they found a banquet set out for forty guests, the meat still roasting over the fire. The ravenous soldiers devoured all the food and wine, then looted the president's home.

One officer took off his grimy, sweat-stained uniform and helped himself to one of the president's fine linen shirts. Finding an old bundle of love letters in Dolley Madison's desk drawer, Admiral Cockburn stuffed them in his pocket, supposedly saying that they would made good reading for those lonely nights at sea. When they had plundered all they pleased, the redcoats set fire to the building.

The red glow of the burning capital was visible as far as Baltimore, forty miles away, until a torrential thunderstorm doused the flames sometime after midnight. The next morning, August 25, Admiral Cockburn had the fires started up again. Around noon, a storm hit the city and helped put out some fires.

Later, while a company of redcoats was destroying a city arsenal, an accidental explosion killed or wounded more than sixty men. (The same thing had happened to General Pike's men at York—a bizarre coincidence.) Having had enough of the inhospitable American capital, General Ross ordered his army back to the fleet that evening. After an exhausting march, the British reembarked at Benedict and sailed off to make their next strike.

The British government later condemned the burning of Washington, although Cockburn's actions had been consistent with the War Office's grand strategy—namely, to bring "hard war" to American soil. Yet its effect was miscalculated. The British had hoped to break the morale of the already war-weary American people. Instead, outraged and insulted, the public now rallied behind the war effort more than ever.

BY THE DAWN'S EARLY LIGHT

The British fleet's next target was Baltimore, the fourth largest city in the United States and home port to a multitude of privateers. Unlike Washington, which was the seat of government but little more, Baltimore was a key industrial and financial center and had many war industries. Its loss would have been a terrible blow.

Yet, also unlike Washington, the citizens of Baltimore rose in defense of their city instead of running away. Men, women, and even children worked long hours digging trenches and constructing breastworks. Volunteers streamed in from the surrounding countryside to join the militia. Baltimore's garrison grew to some 12,000 militiamen (including many Bladensburg veterans), 600 regulars, and 1,000 sailors and marines, commanded by Oliver Hazard Perry.

General Ross took his army ashore about eight miles east of Baltimore on September 12. A force of about 3,000 militiamen marched out of Baltimore to meet the enemy. The Americans harassed Ross's men with sniper fire and fought two skirmishes before retreating back to the city. The British suffered well over three hundred casualties for the day—about double the number for the Americans. Among them was General Ross, who died after a sniper bullet picked him off his white horse. The next day the British scouted

Francis Scott Key glimpses the flag.

out Baltimore's elaborate, cannon-studded defenses. They came to the conclusion that taking the city would be very costly, if possible at all.

Meanwhile, Admiral Cockburn was trying without success to force Fort McHenry—the key to Baltimore's harbor—into surrendering. For twenty-five hours, the British pounded the fort with mortar bombs, cannonballs, and rockets. At dawn on September 14, a Washington lawyer named Francis Scott Key, who was watching the bombardment, was asked by a nearsighted friend if the American flag was still waving over Fort McHenry. The moment captured Key's imagination. Moved, he was inspired to write a poem, which was later put to the tune of an old British drinking song and eventually became "The Star-Spangled Banner," the American national anthem.

Having failed on land and sea, the British packed up and departed Chesapeake Bay. Meanwhile, the second phase of Britain's plan to bring the United States to its knees, the thrust down Lake Champlain, ended almost before it began.

Although the British Army marched into New York with an overwhelming superiority in military manpower and equipment, their advance depended on keeping open their lines of communication and supply. This meant having control of the key inland waterways. But the British Lake Champlain flotilla was destroyed by the Americans at the Battle of Lake Champlain on September 11, 1814, making control of the waterways impossible. The British were forced to scrub the whole operation and pull back to Canada.

Thus in the North as well as the East the war had become a stalemate, with neither side able to achieve a decisive blow. Only in the South was the war still active.

CHAPTER 9

THE WAR IN THE SOUTH

The War of 1812 did not spread to the South until the fall of 1814. Yet that region had been anything but quiet. In the summer of the previous year, a conflict flared up in the Deep South that, although separate, was directly connected to the war with Britain. It was a savage struggle between the white man and the red man, known as the Creek War.

The seeds of this conflict were sown by Tecumseh in 1811, during his visit to the Creek country. Preaching his vision of a united Indian confederation that would stop the whites from further encroachment on tribal lands, Tecumseh won many converts.

When he returned in late 1812, Tecumseh brought more than just his fiery ideas. He could now point to a great military victory. After hearing the dramatic story of how his braves and his British allies had defeated a mighty American army at Detroit, many young Creek warriors rallied behind Tecumseh's cause.

One party of about thirty Upper Creeks, led by a hothead named Little Warrior, even went to Canada and later took part in the River Raisin massacre. On the journey back they killed some American settlers around the mouth of the Ohio River. The United States government was furious with the Creeks, with whom they were supposedly at peace. It demanded these murderers be turned over at once.

The Lower Creeks were anxious not to provoke the United States. They wanted to turn in the culprits, but the Upper Creeks preferred going on the warpath to handing over their brothers to the Americans.

The Council of Creek Elders finally decided to take matters into their own hands. They rounded up Little Warrior and his followers and executed them. They hoped that this would settle the crisis. Sadly, it had the reverse effect—it plunged the Creek nation into a bloody civil war. Order was finally restored by a militant group of young Upper Creek warriors, called Red Sticks because of their crimson stone-headed war clubs.

In July 1813, British agents in Pensacola, a major outpost in Spanish Florida, arranged for the Spanish authorities to give the Red Sticks firearms and ammunition. (The governor of Florida claimed they were for "hunting purposes" only.) On the return trip, the Indians were met by a band of angry white settlers at a place called Burnt Corn, about eighty miles north of Pensacola. Most of the Indians escaped, but much of their shipment was captured.

Outraged, the Red Sticks made plans for revenge. On August 30, eight hundred braves gathered in the woods around Fort Mims, a stockade about sixty miles northwest of Pensacola in Mississippi Territory. Just as the garrison was sitting down to the noon meal, the Red Sticks broke cover and stormed through an open gate. Of the 175 militiamen and about four hundred civilians, only seventeen people escaped. The rest—men, women, and children—were killed or enslaved.

OLD HICKORY The Fort Mims Massacre sent a shiver through the American people. The settlers along the frontier, naturally, were most alarmed. A force of about 3,500 Tennessee and Mississippi volunteers and a regiment of Army regulars was hastily assembled in Nashville to deal with the Creek menace.

The man picked to lead the expedition was an uncultured, slave-owning, frontier-bred Indian-fighter who would go on to become the seventh, and least educated, president of the United States. That man was Andrew Jackson. Jackson was a major general in the Tennessee State Militia. He had a reputation as a tough and able military leader, both feared and respected by his men.

Jackson was not a handsome man. His body was bony and weatherbeaten. His face was pitted from smallpox and punctuated with a long scar that ran down his forehead and onto his left cheek. His gun-metal blue eyes shot cold stares to friend and foe alike. Jackson seldom smiled and had little sense of humor. Because of his hardwood temperament and his wood-hard stamina, his men had nicknamed him "Old Hickory."

At the time he was called on to take command, Jackson was bedridden and near death. He had been shot during a wild tavern brawl with the Benton brothers of Missouri. (The man who shot him was Thomas Hart Benton, a future U.S. senator.) Never one to pass up a call to arms, he accepted the command—only death could have stopped Andrew Jackson. With his arm in a sling and Benton's bullet still lodged in his shoulder, Jackson marched off with his army in October.

He had no illusions about what lay ahead. Although the recent civil war had left the Creek nation in a weakened condition, they were still a well-organized, resourceful, and resilient people. Jackson knew that to defeat the Creeks, he would have to destroy their capacity to resist. This meant burning their villages and crops and killing their livestock. It was a black and ugly task. Old Hickory was the right man for the job.

(Jackson's selection for command was probably based on his superb military ability; but his callous disregard for the lives of Indians was well known, and that may have influenced the decision. Later, as president, Jackson's policies

*Andrew Jackson as a major general
during the War of 1812.*

toward the Indians, including their forced "resettlement," would become one of the darkest and most shameful episodes in American history.)

War against the Creeks meant that Jackson and his men would have to cross some of the most rugged, untamed wilderness in the world, a landscape that the enemy knew intimately. The march through Creek country was an ordeal of chest-deep, snake-infested swamps, dense forests, and mountainous terrain. To add to the soldiers' discomfort, there were stinging horseflies, biting lice, and blood-sucking mosquitoes, leeches, and ticks, along with poison ivy and tooth-leafed nettles.

Then the food ran out. The Americans had to eat berries, roots, acorns, and even tree bark. General Jackson took no special privileges, enduring everything his men did. His suffering was even worse because of his throbbing shoulder. He also came down with dysentery, a painful form of diarrhea.

As well as these hardships, the soldiers had to face numerous fights against whooping, war-painted Indians. Yet for all his fanatical courage, the Creek brave was no match for the American soldier. With few muskets and no artillery, the Creeks fought a losing, running struggle against Jackson's superior weapons and fire tactics.

On November 3, 1813, about 180 Red Sticks were killed at the Battle of Tullushatchee, while American casualties were five dead and fourteen wounded. Six days later another three hundred Creek warriors were killed at the Battle of Talladega. As the months passed, Old Hickory and his army penetrated deeper and deeper into the Creek homeland, ravaging the country as they went. Along the way they built three forts and fought more hard-to-pronounce battles—Econochaca, Autossee, Emackfau, Tuckabatchee.

The knockout blow came on March 27, 1814, along a U-shaped bend in the Tallapoosa River in the heart of Creek country. There Jackson found about eight hundred Red Sticks who had set up a fortified position, waiting to make

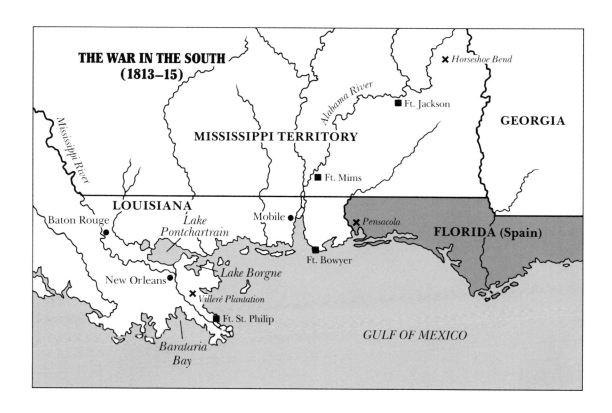

THE WAR IN THE SOUTH
(1813–15)

× Horseshoe Bend

Alabama River

■ Ft. Jackson

GEORGIA

Mississippi River

MISSISSIPPI TERRITORY

■ Ft. Mims

LOUISIANA

Baton Rouge

Lake Pontchartrain

Mobile ●

× Pensacola

FLORIDA (Spain)

New Orleans ●

Lake Borgne

■ Ft. Bowyer

× Villeré Plantation

■ Ft. St. Philip

Barataria Bay

GULF OF MEXICO

a final stand. Protected on three sides by water, the Indians had built across their front a wall of thick pine logs, five to eight feet tall.

Jackson spent the morning trying to breach the wall with his artillery, but most of the cannonballs bounced off the logs. About noon he ordered a frontal assault.

The first man to mount the barricade was killed instantly. The second man, a young officer named Sam Houston, jumped down on the Indians, swinging his sword like a madman. (Houston was twice wounded but survived to become the governor of Tennessee and first president of the Republic of Texas.) Not far behind him was Davy Crockett (who would later fight at the Alamo).

Once they were past the wall, the Americans closed a tight ring around the Indians. Jackson, seeing the battle won, offered the Red Sticks generous terms of surrender. They refused, and the slaughter went on into dusk. "We shot them like dogs," recalled Crockett.[25] Of the original eight hundred or so defenders, probably not more than two dozen escaped. Forty-nine of Jackson's men were killed and 157 wounded.

Following the Battle of Horseshoe Bend, General Jackson and his army easily mopped up the remaining pockets of Creek resistance. The Creeks were stunned by Jackson's harsh peace terms, but they had no choice but to accept them. On August 9, 1814, Creek representatives signed a treaty at the newly built Fort Jackson, which ceded 23 million acres of land (one fifth of Georgia and three fifths of what was later Alabama) to the United States.

THE PENSACOLA OPERATION

The U.S. government considered the end of the Creek War to be the end of the war on the southern front. It instructed General Jackson to disband his force. Old Hickory, however, knew better. He had received intelligence reports of British troops and ships gathering at Pensacola. Jackson suspected, correctly, that they were the vanguard of a large invasion force.

Andrew Jackson despised Englishmen even more than Indians. He had lost his mother and both his brothers in the War of Independence. Although only a boy of thirteen, young Andy had fought in several skirmishes against the redcoats. The scar on his face had come from the sword of a British lieutenant when he refused to clean the officer's boots, and the pockmarks from smallpox he caught while in a British prison camp.

Jackson now feared that the British were planning to take Mobile, a port fifty miles west of Pensacola. Mobile's deepwater harbor made it an ideal staging area for a drive inland. From there, New Orleans could be cut off and captured. On August 27, Jackson dispatched troops and heavy cannons to strengthen Fort Bowyer, which guarded the entrance to Mobile Bay. His suspicion proved correct.

On September 15, four British warships tried to sail into the bay, two passing Fort Bowyer at pistol range, while a force of Royal Marines that had landed earlier attempted to storm the fort from the rear. The Americans drove off both attacks. The British squadron had to return to Pensacola without its flagship, which was shot up so badly that it had to be abandoned and burned.

Furious that the Spanish authorities had allowed the British to use their territory as a base of operations, General Jackson prepared to invade Florida at once. Spain, although allied with Britain, was officially neutral during the War of 1812. Jackson asked Washington for permission to carry out his attack, but authorization was never sent. Having grown impatient with the delay, he marched into Florida with approximately 4,000 men. (The government had, in fact, sent a letter, dated October 28, 1814, strictly forbidding any trespass of Spanish territory; but Jackson claimed he did not receive it until after the war.)

In November, the Americans captured Pensacola after some heavy fighting. The British were forced to evacuate their men and ships. After blowing up the forts surrounding the city and a British munitions depot in Apalachicola, Jackson marched his men back to Mobile.

Deprived of bases on the Gulf coast, the British had to assemble their invasion force in Jamaica. From there they planned their next move.

THE PEACE TALKS Meanwhile, halfway across the globe, an Anglo-American peace conference was in progress at the city of Ghent in Belgium. Months earlier the United States had offered to sign a peace treaty on the basis of *status quo ante bellum,* meaning the way that everything was before the war.

The British, still flush with excitement over their great triumph in Europe, had refused. The attitude of the British government and the British people had been that the Americans should first get a good drubbing and then be forced to give up large amounts of territory for all the trouble they'd caused Britain.

This feeling changed dramatically when the news reached England that the British forces had retreated from New York and been repulsed at Baltimore. These were major setbacks. They meant that winning the war, even if still possible, would take at least another year, at tremendous cost. On top of this, the commerce-raiding American privateers were taking an increasingly heavy toll on Britain's economy.

Now all the British people wanted was peace. The British government was also anxious to sign a treaty, but it still hoped for some territorial gains from the United States. The Americans, naturally, thought this was outrageous. So, too, did many Englishmen.

Only months earlier the London *Times* had clamored for revenge on the United States, writing: "Chastise the savages, for such they are!"[26] Now *The Times* published articles protesting the greedy and unrealistic demands of the British government.

Even the Duke of Wellington, the greatest British commander of the age and future hero of Waterloo, when asked for his opinion by the British Cabinet, sent a bleak response. He said that a military solution did not look promising and suggested that they accept the American proposal for ante-bellum status quo. He ended his reply by saying:

> *You have no right . . . to demand any concession of territory. . . . The state of your military operations . . . does not entitle you to any.*[27]

Yet the Ghent negotiations dragged on into December as the British continued to haggle with the American delegation over nit-picking terms. The British delegates were stalling, hoping to receive news of a great victory at New Orleans, thinking it might strengthen their hand at the negotiating table.

THE BATTLE OF NEW ORLEANS

The surest way to take New Orleans was to place a force just to the north of the city, preventing supplies and reinforcements from reaching it. This move would also trap the defending American force, which otherwise could escape up the Mississippi in barges with most of their equipment and supplies and all the valuables and riches of New Orleans.

Of course, such a plan meant that the British Army would have to march overland across Mississippi Territory. This was impossible without a good base on the Gulf coast. Therefore, the logical step was still to take Mobile first, as originally planned. The worst thing the British could do would be to try to take New Orleans directly from the sea. From a military standpoint, it was highly impractical. There were a dozen ways to defend the city from an amphibious invasion. The Duke of Wellington himself strongly advised against a direct assault. Yet this was precisely what the British set out to do.

When General Jackson received word from his spies that the British invasion fleet had left Jamaica and was heading toward the Mississippi River delta, he left at once for New Orleans. Just in case these reports proved incorrect, he left a substantial garrison at Mobile. He sent the bulk of his remaining force to Baton Rouge, from where it could be rushed to either point if need be.

Jackson arrived at New Orleans on December 1, 1814. The next day the town gentry prepared an elegant reception banquet for the homely, stone-faced Tennessee general, but Jackson had no time for such fanciful frivolity.* He had already begun working to improve the city's defenses and organize its people.

New Orleans was situated on the east bank of the Mississippi, about a hundred miles from the mouth of the river. Except for a narrow strip of dry land just east of the city, it was surrounded on all sides for miles around by dense, impassible swampland. There were several ways to approach the city from the Gulf of Mexico, but none were

---

*Jackson would have to pass up many a fine dinner. His digestive system had been irreversibly damaged while he was serving his country in the Creek War. The whole time he was in New Orleans, boiled rice was about the only thing his stomach could hold down.

easy. One way was to pass through Barataria Bay, an intricate waterway south of the city that was understood only by the pirates who lived there. The British offered to pay the Baratarian pirates handsomely if they would help, but they refused. Instead, this merry band of outlaws, led by the Lafitte brothers, Jean and Pierre, offered their invaluable services to General Jackson free of charge.

Another route to the city was up the winding Mississippi, which was guarded by Fort Bourbon, Fort St. Philip, and Fort St. Leon. Even though these forts ordinarily would have presented a very difficult obstacle, Old Hickory had improved them so well that now they would be virtually impossible to get by. Jackson also rejuvenated Fort St. John, north of the city, making the passage through Lake Pontchartrain an equally poor option for the British.

The only choice left was Lake Borgne, east of the city. Because the coastal sound was too shallow for warships, the British would have to drop anchor about thirty miles from the opening of the lake and send the troops out in rowboats. Then they would have to row another thirty miles across Lake Borgne to the western shore. From there they would have to explore a reptile-laden labyrinth of marshy, reed-choked creeks, or bayous, in hope of finding one that led to open ground.

General Jackson managed to have a few bayous rendered impassable and posted guards along others. In addition, Lake Borgne was patrolled by five small American gunboats that should have provided early warning of enemy activity in the lake. But the British sent out forty-five rowboats, loaded down with 1,200 sailors and marines, to capture the five gunboats on the night of December 12. Outnumbered nine to one in men and boats, the Americans fled to warn General Jackson. Unfortunately, wind conditions were not favorable. After a grueling thirty-six-hour chase, the hard-rowing British caught up to and captured the American flotilla.

It took seven more exhausting days for the British seamen to row the rest of the invasion force from the fleet to the west end of Lake Borgne. Without shelter, exposed to freezing December rains, the perpetually wet redcoats suffered terribly. About a thousand were put out of action by the weather and returned to the fleet.

On December 22, a British scout discovered an unobstructed and unguarded bayou that led to a sugar plantation named Villeré, a few miles southeast of New Orleans. General Jackson had, in fact, issued written orders to block this bayou. Why this had not been done remains a mystery. By noon the following day, an advance spearhead of about 2,400 redcoats under General John Keane poured out of the swamp and into Villeré Plantation.

The British had managed to catch the Americans off guard. Had General Keane attacked that afternoon, he might have overwhelmed Jackson, who probably had no more than 2,100 men at his disposal. Keane, however, knew his soaked-to-the-bone troops had not had a full night's sleep or a hot meal in a week. He decided to rest his men and wait until morning.

But a full night's rest for the enemy was not on General Jackson's agenda. Although he was thunderstruck when he learned that the British had penetrated his defenses undetected, Jackson did not hesitate a moment. He marshaled his forces and prepared to launch a night raid on the British camp. About 6:30 P.M., while the unsuspecting redcoats were stretching out around their campfires and drying their uniforms, General Jackson began moving down the east bank of the Mississippi with some 2,000 men.

The American force was a colorful hodgepodge of troops. The stiff-collared blue jackets of U.S. Army regulars could be seen alongside the brown shirts of Tennessee marksmen and the flashy red, blue, and gold uniforms of the local Creole militia. There were even a few French soldiers who had fought for Napoleon.

Jackson's force also included two battalions of free blacks and a group of friendly Choctaw Indians, led by Chief Push-Ma-Ta-Ha. These units would contribute much to the American cause. To his credit, General Jackson insisted that all his men be paid the same "whether the troops are white, black, or tea."[28]

The Americans attacked at 8 P.M. The sharp struggle that followed was mainly fought hand to hand with bayonets, hunting knives, and tomahawks. An hour later the British began to push the Americans back. At 9:30, Jackson ordered a retreat. He left behind 213 of his men killed, wounded, or captured.

Although General Keane's casualties were only about a dozen more than those of the Americans, he was badly shaken by Jackson's sudden attack. No commander, he reasoned, would throw 2,000 men into a risky night action unless he had thousands more in reserve. Convinced that Jackson possessed a much larger force, Keane licked his wounds and waited for the main body of the British force to arrive.

Having bought the time he needed, Jackson took up a position a couple of miles west of the enemy. His men spent all the next day, Christmas Eve, digging in.

That same day, December 24, 1814, British and American negotiators signed a document declaring the restoration of the pre-war state of Anglo-American affairs and the formal end of hostilities between the United States and Great Britain, effective immediately. The Treaty of Ghent made no mention of neutral rights, free trade, or impressment, but it confirmed U.S. control of the Northwest. At last, the War of 1812 was over.

Of course, it would take weeks for even the fastest sailing ship to bring this news of peace to America. A needless battle, the biggest and bloodiest of the war, would yet be fought. By December 27, the British had over 6,000 troops assembled at Villeré Plantation and were ready to move. The next morning they advanced toward the American line.

General Jackson was ready for them. His line extended three quarters of a mile, from the edge of a cypress swamp on the left to the bank of the Mississippi on the right. Along its entire length stretched a strong defensive rampart constructed from logs, earth, and thick bales of cotton. In front

Signing the Treaty of Ghent.

of this wall was a ditch four feet deep and ten feet wide.
Along the wall at regular intervals were large-caliber naval
guns manned by the Lafittes' skilled, highly accurate pirate
gunners. In addition, the reinforcements from Baton Rouge
had arrived, bringing Jackson's total strength up to about
5,200 men.

After a very brief attack, the British retired to Villeré.
Blaming their failure on a lack of artillery, they decided
that naval guns would have to be hauled in from the fleet
sixty miles away. It took hundreds of men three backbreaking days to transport the guns. Each soldier was ordered to
carry back a cannonball in his knapsack. One unlucky squad
of cannonball-encumbered redcoats disappeared forever
beneath Lake Borgne when their rowboat capsized.

Concealed by early morning fog, the British guns were
secretly put in position opposite the American line on New

Year's Day. When the fog lifted, a furious artillery duel began. The American guns, although outnumbered twenty-four to fifteen, gradually tore apart the enemy batteries. At noon the British retreated.

Over the next few days the British received some reinforcements that brought their total strength to just over 9,000 troops. The next attack would be all-out. The soldiers did everything they could to prepare for the final assault. They fashioned scaling ladders out of wood and bundled together sugarcane stalks that would be used to fill the ditch.

At daybreak on January 8, 1815, Britain's finest regiments advanced across the flat, muddy field straight at the American line like lambs to the slaughter. Their clean white cross belts made perfect targets for Jackson's Kentucky riflemen. The terrible carnage that followed is remembered

At New Orleans, the British marched in close ranks against positions defended by Jackson's artillery and riflemen.

as the Battle of New Orleans. According to the refrain of a popular American song of the same name, it went something like this:

We fired our guns and the British kept-a-comin',
There wasn't as many as there was a while ago.
We fired once more and they began-a-runnin',
Down the Mississippi to the Gulf of Mexico.

Well, it was more complicated than that, but not much. The British infantry charged repeatedly but were cut to pieces by the relentless American fire. A few redcoats actually made it up to the wall, but none made it over. When their lines began to disintegrate, the British were forced to give up the attack. It was all over by 8:30 A.M.

Britain's casualties for that morning were 2,036 men, including three generals. Another five hundred were captured. Jackson's losses were seven men killed and six wounded.

THE HARTFORD CONVENTION

Andrew Jackson had won the greatest military contest on American soil since the Battle of Yorktown thirty-four years earlier. Yet even as Westerners and Southerners were fighting for their country in the New Orleans campaign, a shameful episode was taking place in New England.

Many New Englanders had continued their opposition to the war. While the economy stagnated in the rest of the country, there were many greedy profiteers who grew fat from their treasonous trade with Britain. The British Army probably could not have remained in Canada had it not been consistently supplied and fed by Vermont contractors.

The worst act of treason came when Massachusetts sent out an appeal to neighboring states for a conference to discuss the idea of seceding from the United States and signing a peace treaty with Britain. State delegates from Massachusetts, Connecticut, and Rhode Island and delegates from a few counties in Vermont and New Hampshire met secretly in Hartford, Connecticut, from December 1814 to January 1815.

It is fortunate for the United States that the British negotiators at Ghent were not aware of the Hartford Convention. Had they known that the long-awaited crack in the wall of American unity had finally appeared, they might have pressed for concessions or even continued the war.

The delegates at Hartford sent three "ambassadors" to Washington to demand changes in the Constitution. But their arrival in the capital was blotted out by the good news from New Orleans. The psychological effect this great American victory had on the public was enormous. The whole country was swept up in a frenzied wave of celebration and joy. And defeatist attitudes that may have been smoldering among the people were now swept away by a tide of nationalist feeling.

A week later, on February 14, 1815, a copy of the Treaty of Ghent reached Washington. The matter of the Hartford Convention was quietly and quickly dismissed. Both the convention members and the U.S. government thought the whole incident best forgotten. At last the nation was at peace again. The United States had not won the war but had not lost it, either. As in the War of Independence a generation earlier, America emerged from a struggle for its very existence united and free.

The Boston Evening Gazette *announced news of the treaty in February 1815.*

EPILOGUE

The peace celebrations in Washington had scarcely ended when Congress once again declared war—on Algiers. For no sooner had American merchant ships returned to the Mediterranean than the Algerines began attacking them again.

Commodore Stephen Decatur was dispatched at once with a squadron of warships (including the former British frigate *Macedonian*) to suppress the new outbreak of piracy. After capturing the flagship of the Algerine Navy, Decatur sailed into the harbor of Algiers. Anxious to save his capital and the rest of his fleet from destruction, the pasha agreed to release all captives and never demand tribute again. In addition, Decatur made the pasha pay for the cost of the American expedition. On June 30, 1815, a treaty was signed ending the war with Algiers.

The American squadron then proceeded to Tunis and Tripoli, where Commodore Decatur forced similar treaties on the rulers. The agreements included the release of all Christian captives regardless of nationality. Stephen Decatur was indeed a remarkable man. Had he not been killed in a duel in 1820, he would have almost certainly entered politics. He might have even become the first Navy man to be elected president.

Having settled the unfinished business with the Barbary States, America began a long period of peace, coupled with a stronger-than-ever sense of national pride. Prosperity followed, too, partly as a result of the war. For during the three years in which the United States was cut off from British manufactured goods, Americans were forced to do their own manufacturing. The new industries they forged were the driving force behind America's postwar economic boom.

Another significant effect of the war was that it effectively isolated the Indian nations. Never again would Britain or any other power intercede on the Indians' behalf or treat them as sovereign peoples. The question of the fate of Native Americans was now an internal affair to be handled exclusively by the United States.

Thus the United States emerged from the War of 1812 stronger than ever. The war paved the way for rapid expansion and marked the beginning of the next major chapter of U.S. history—the opening of the American West.

THE WAR OF 1812

IMPORTANT DATES

1783	Treaty of Paris ends Revolutionary War.
1787	U.S. Constitution adopted.
1794	Jay's Treaty signed with Britain.
1797	*Constitution* launched in Boston harbor.
1798–1800	Undeclared naval war with France.
1801–05	Tripolitan War.
1807	Britain issues Orders-in-Council.
	Chesapeake-Leopard affair.
	President Jefferson signs Embargo Act.
1811	Battle of Tippecanoe.

1812

June 18	United States declares war on Britain.
Aug. 16	Detroit surrenders.
Aug. 19	*Constitution* defeats the *Guerrière*.
Oct. 12	American Army routed at the Battle of Queenston Heights.
Oct. 29	*United States* defeats the *Macedonian*.
Dec. 29	*Constitution* defeats the *Java*.

1813

Jan. 22	River Raisin Massacre.
April 27	American Army sacks York, burns Parliament buildings.
June 1	*Shannon* defeats the *Chesapeake.*
Aug. 30	Fort Mims Massacre.
Sept. 10	Perry wins Battle of Lake Erie.
Oct. 5	Tecumseh killed at Battle of Thames River.

1814

March 27	General Jackson defeats the last of the Red Sticks at Battle of Horseshoe Bend.
April 12	Napoleon abdicates.
July 5	American victory at Battle of Chippewa.
Aug. 9	Treaty of Fort Jackson ends Creek War.
Aug. 24–25	British burn Washington.
Sept. 11	British defeated at Battle of Lake Champlain and forced to return to Canada.
Sept. 12–13	British repulsed at Baltimore.
Nov. 7	General Jackson takes Pensacola.
Dec. 24	Treaty of Ghent signed.

1815

Jan. 8	Battle of New Orleans.

NOTES

The account of the fight between the *United States* and the
Macedonian in chapter 1 is based on the memoirs of Samuel
Leach, a midshipman aboard the *Macedonian*. Leach told
the story of the battle in his book *Thirty Years from Home*,
which was published in the 1840s. Much of the dialogue
and some of the descriptions have been added to the ver-
sion that appears here.

Following are source notes for quotations that appear else-
where in this book.

1. E. B. Potter, *The Naval Academy Illustrated History of the
   United States Navy* (New York: Galahad Books, 1971),
   p. 28.
2. Robert Leckie, *The Wars of America* (New York: Harper
   and Row, 1968), p. 225.
3. Quoted in Fletcher Pratt, *Compact History of the United
   States Navy* (New York: Hawthorne Books, 1967), p. 56.

4. Quoted in Edward L. Beach, *The United States Navy: 200 Years* (New York: Henry Holt and Company, 1986), p. 33.
5. Quoted in Beach, p. 44.
6. Quoted in William M. Fowler, *Jack Tars & Commodores: The American Navy 1783 to 1815* (Boston: Houghton Mifflin Company, 1984), p. 101.
7. Leckie, p. 230.
8. Quoted in Albert Marrin, *1812: The War Nobody Won* (New York: Atheneum, 1985), p. 12.
9. Beach, p. 62.
10. Beach, p. 63.
11. Beach, p. 64.
12. Quoted in Fawn N. Brodie, *Thomas Jefferson, an Intimate History* (New York: W. W. Norton & Co. Inc., 1974), p. 416.
13. Leckie, p. 237.
14. Harry L. Coles, *The War of 1812* (Chicago: Chicago University Press, 1965), p. 80.
15. Coles, p. 81.
16. Quoted in Leckie, p. 250.
17. Quoted in Coles, p. 84.
18. Quoted in Ralph D. Paine, *The Fight for a Free Sea* (New Haven: Yale University Press, 1920), p. 123.
19. Clifford Lindsey Alderman, *The Privateersmen* (Philadelphia: Chilton Books, 1965).
20. Marrin, p. 40.
21. Leckie, p. 262.
22. Quoted in Coles, p. 121.
23. Quoted in John Garraty, *The American Nation, Vol. 1* (1975), p. 185.
24. Quoted in Richard Dillon, *We Have Met the Enemy* (New York: McGraw Hill, 1978), p. 153.
25. Quoted in Marrin, p. 147.
26. Leckie, p. 298.
27. Leckie, p. 299.
28. Quoted in Marrin, p. 151.

GLOSSARY

Barbary Coast—a region of North Africa extending from west of Egypt to the Atlantic Ocean comprising, in the 1800s, the four pirate-infested Barbary States: Morocco, Algiers, Tunis, and Tripoli.

boom—a spar on which the bottom of a triangular sail is fastened.

bowsprit—a large spar projecting forward from the bow of a ship.

breastwork—a hastily constructed fortification, usually chest-high.

brig—a two-masted warship usually mounting between 10 and 20 guns.

broadside—all the guns that can be fired from one side of a warship, or a simultaneous discharge of all the guns on one side of a warship.

carronade—a stubby, swivel-mounted cannon that fired a massive cannonball but was effective only at very short ranges. (The name comes from the foundry that invented and manufactured them, the Carron company of Scotland.)

cat-o'-nine-tails—a whip with nine knotted cords fastened to a handle, used to flog offenders.

contraband—smuggled goods.

crossing the T—a tactical nautical maneuver in which one warship's broadside faces the bow of the enemy vessel.

flank—the extreme right or left side of an army.

flotilla—a small fleet.

frigate—a warship with a single gun deck, mounting between 30 and 50 guns, with three masts: the fore (first), main (second), and mizzen (third) masts.

gaff—a spar on which the top of a sail is fastened.

jib—a triangular sail extending from the foremast to the bowsprit of a ship.

ketch—a small vessel with one large mast, usually rigged with a triangular sail.

militia—armed forces made up of citizens and called up in emergencies.

mortar boat—a vessel that carries a mortar (a massive cannon designed to fire shells at high angles).

privateer—a privately owned and manned armed vessel, commissioned by a government in time of war to fight the enemy.

regular—a full-time, professional soldier, a member of a standing army.

rigging—the ropes, chains, masts, yards, etc., used to support and work the sails on a ship.

ship of the line—a battleship with two to three gun decks, mounting between 60 and 120 guns.

spanker—a sail on the mast nearest the stern of a square-rigged ship.

top yards—spars for carrying a ship's topsails (the second lowest sails on a square-rigged ship).

THE WAR OF 1812

FOR FURTHER READING

The Battle of Lake Erie by F. Van Wyck Mason (Boston: Houghton Mifflin Company, 1960).

The Battle of New Orleans by Donald Barr Childsey (New York: Crown Publishing, 1961).

The Battles of the Constitution by Robert Goldston (Toronto: Collier-Macmillan Company, 1969).

The Burning of Washington by John Phelan (New York: Thomas Y. Crowell Company, 1975).

The Commodore's Boys: The Naval Campaigns of the War of 1812 by Helen Orlob (Philadelphia: Westminster Press, 1967).

The Cruise of the Essex by Irving Werstein (Philadelphia: Macrae Smith Company, 1969).

The Naval War with France 1798–1800 by David C. Knight (New York: Franklin Watts, Inc., 1970).

The Privateersmen by Clifford Lindsey Alderman (Philadelphia: Chilton Books, 1965).

The War Nobody Won: 1812 by Robert Leckie (New York: G. P. Putnam's Sons, 1974).

Wooden Ships and Iron Men by Clifford Lindsey Alderman (New York: Walker and Company, 1964).

BIBLIOGRAPHY

Alderman, Clifford Lindsey. *The Privateersmen*. Philadelphia: Chilton Books, 1965.

Alderman, Clifford Lindsey. *Wooden Ships and Iron Men*. New York: Walker and Company, 1964.

Beach, Edward L. *The United States Navy: 200 Years*. New York: Henry Holt and Company, 1986.

Caffrey, Kate. *The Twilight's Last Gleaming*. New York: Stein and Day, 1977.

Coles, Harry L. *The War of 1812*. Chicago: Chicago University Press, 1965.

Fowler, William M., Jr. *Jack Tars & Commodores: The American Navy 1783 to 1815*. Boston: Houghton Mifflin Company, 1984.

Goldston, Robert. *The Battles of the Constitution*. Toronto: Collier-Macmillan Company, 1969.

Hart, Albert, editor. *American History Told by Contemporaries*, Volume III. New York: Macmillan and Company, 1901.

Horsman, Reginald. *The War of 1812*. New York: Alfred Knopf, 1969.

Leckie, Robert. *The War Nobody Won: 1812*. New York: G. P. Putnam's Sons, 1974.

Leckie, Robert. *The Wars of America*. New York: Harper and Row, 1968.

Lord, Walter. *The Dawn's Early Light*. New York: W. W. Norton and Company, 1972.

Marrin, Albert. *1812: The War Nobody Won*. New York: Atheneum, 1985.

Morrison, Samuel. *Dissent in Three American Wars*. Cambridge: Harvard University Press, 1970.

Phelan, John. *The Burning of Washington*. New York: Thomas Y. Crowell Company, 1975.

Potter, E. B. *The Naval Academy Illustrated History of the United States Navy*. New York: Galahad Books, 1971.

Tucker, Glenn. *Poltroons and Patriots*. Indianapolis: Bobbs-Merrill Company, 1954.

Werstein, Irving. *The Cruise of the Essex*. Philadelphia: Macrae Smith Company, 1969.

INDEX